W9-ABT-781

Ancient Civilizations of the New World

Essays in World History

William H. McNeill and Ross E. Dunn, Series Editors

Ancient Civilizations of the New World

Richard E. W. Adams
University of Texas at San Antonio

WestviewPress
A Division of HarperCollins*Publishers*

Essays in World History

All rights reserved. Printed in the United States of America. No part of this publication may be reproduced or transmitted in any form or by any means, electronic or mechanical, including photocopy, recording, or any information storage and retrieval system, without permission in writing from the publisher.

Copyright © 1997 by Westview Press, A Division of HarperCollins Publishers, Inc.

Published in 1997 in the United States of America by Westview Press, 5500 Central Avenue, Boulder, Colorado 80301-2877, and in the United Kingdom by Westview Press, 12 Hid's Copse Road, Cumnor Hill, Oxford OX2 9JJ

Library of Congress Cataloging-in-Publication Data
Adams, Richard E. W., 1931–
    Ancient civilizations of the New World / Richard E.W. Adams.
        p.   cm.—(Essays in world history)
    Includes bibliographical references and index.
    ISBN 0-8133-1382-1 (hc).—ISBN 0-8133-1383-X (pbk)
    1. Indians of Mexico—Antiquities.   2. Mexico—Antiquities.
3. Indians of Central America—Antiquities.   4. Central America—
Antiquities.   5. Indians of South America—Antiquities.   6. South
America—Antiquities.   I. Title.   II. Series.
F1219.7.A33   1997
980'.012—dc21   97-15752
                                                                                      CIP

The paper used in this publication meets the requirements of the American National Standard for Permanence of Paper for Printed Library Materials Z39.48-1984.

10   9   8   7   6   5   4   3   2   1

To the memory of my grandparents,
Charles K. Wood and Mary K. Wood

Contents

Tables and Illustrations

Acknowledgments

The duty of acknowledging intellectual and other debts incurred in the writing of this book is a pleasant task. One can recognize many people who have contributed directly to the immediate book and also thank others less directly—though no less importantly—involved in one's intellectual journey. First, I must thank the editors of this series, William McNeill and Ross Dunn, for their forbearance, encouragement, and not least, their courage. René Millon, Rebecca Gonzalez Lauck, Jeremy Sabloff, Michael Moseley, and Craig Morris all furnished permission to reproduce badly needed maps and site plans. My gratitude to them all for their collegiality and generosity. A figure that lies behind nearly all my work in archaeology is my former graduate advisor and always colleague, Gordon R. Willey. His broad interests, profound knowledge, and comparative skills have encouraged me to attempt to emulate him in different ways. Finally, I must acknowledge the constant and unstinting support of my wife, Jane Jackson Adams, who I trust will be pleased with this latest result of an intellectual partnership that has lasted over forty years.

Richard E. W. Adams

1

Introduction:
Complex Cultures, Cities, and a Rapid Survey of the Earliest Old World Civilizations

During the morning, we arrived at a broad causeway and continued our march towards Iztapalapa, and when we saw so many cities and villages built in the water and other great towns on dry land and that straight and level causeway going towards Mexico, we were amazed and said that it was like the enchantments they tell of in the legend of Amadis, on account of the great towers and cues [temples] and buildings rising from the water, and all built of masonry. And some of the soldiers even asked whether the things we saw were not a dream.

Bernal Diaz del Castillo,
The Discovery and Conquest of Mexico, *1956*

In many of the Inca's houses there were large halls some two hundred paces in length and fifty to sixty in breadth. They were unpartitioned and served as places of assembly for festivals and dances when the weather was too rainy to permit them to hold these in the open air. In the city of Cuzco I saw four of these halls, which were still standing when I was a boy . . . and the largest was that of the Cassana, which was capable of holding three thousand people.

Garcilaso de la Vega,
Royal Commentaries of the Incas, *1966*

Bernal Diaz was a product of the European Renaissance and had seen the grand cities of Moorish Spain. He was not easily impressed, but the first sight of the great Aztec capital overwhelmed him and his comrades with its extraordinary setting and grandeur. He retained this sense of wonder at what they had seen and done for the next sixty years of his long life and transmitted it to us by way of his memoirs, written in his old age. Similarly, the Spanish conquerors of the Inca realm, eleven years later, experienced difficulty in comprehending such a different and yet remarkable cultural tradition. As the colonial period continued through 350 years, and as the mixture of Iberian and Native American cultures produced a new set of civilizations, memories and information about the original high cultures were largely reduced to the status of legend or myth, and the achievements of the natives were discounted and denigrated. However, eyewitness accounts survived, both of the conquest itself and of the native cultures. Spanish churchmen were largely responsible for writing about the latter, but even these books and manuscripts were relegated to dusty archives in Spain or to decrepit monastic repositories and libraries in Spain's former colonies, the new national states of Latin America.

Fortunately, historical research and archaeological work of the last 150 years have enabled us to recover a great deal of what seemed irretrievably lost—for instance, information on periods so remote that even the six-teenth-century Native American descendants had lost track of what had happened. This book is intended to present a synthesis of some of the new information now available about the two New World areas of civilized so-cieties. It is by no means exhaustive, and it may not be agreeable to many specialists. However, it is hoped that the book will provide a summary of most of the important happenings in the prehistoric past as well as of per-spectives given us by comparison with Old World civilizations and vari-ous theoretical views. Before going farther, it is necessary to define the concepts of culture and civilization.

New World archaeologists are trained as anthropologists, which means that we share with the social anthropologists a great many common views. One of the most basic is that of culture itself. Cultures are composed of traditional patterned behaviors that are systemically related and that are transmitted from generation to generation in a social group. The many components of cultures may be broken down as institutions. Major cul-tural institutions common to all cultures, no matter how simplified, in-clude kinship, social structure, associations, economics, ideology (includ-ing religion), legal systems, and political systems. All cultures have sets of motivating beliefs; some have called these "core values." The belief in the superiority of social status achieved by individual effort (as opposed to inheritance) is a typical core value in the United States. For the purposes of this book, it should be pointed out that patterned behavior often leaves material traces. Traditional houses built of adobe or stone will still be detectable centuries after they fall down. Varying social statuses are often reflected in the different styles of housing found in an ancient community, with the rich living in larger and better-made structures, and most people dwelling in smaller houses made of less costly materials.

As a field, archaeology has inherent limitations. We cannot observe an ancient culture in action. Everything is over—the people are dead and buried; their houses, temples, workshops, markets, defenses, roads, and the like have deteriorated into ruins. Therefore, an archaeologist must reconstruct a culture by means of the tools, pottery, and other artifacts that are excavated. Buildings, caves, trash heaps, and many other sites are places that will yield data. Not all information can be picked up or photographed, so data on matters such as ancient climate or the patterns of farmhouses in the ancient countryside are very useful. In the end, however, an archaeologist must interpret what is found and then reconstruct what appears to be the most likely series of events to produce the patterns in the data. Only then, when fieldwork is done, can patterns be defined and analyzed and explanations offered. Explanation, or theory, must try to make clear all the patterned information and the exceptions to it. For example, we know that the ancient Maya civilization collapsed, as have many other civilizations. We now understand why this happened to the Maya, and part of our confidence in the explanation is that similar events happened elsewhere. However, as we will see, the Maya did not make a demographic or cultural recovery, something that is very unusual in world history and prehistory. Therefore, our explanation in this case must also cover the unique aspect of this event.

Cultures can be as simple as those hunters and gatherers living in deserts or the Arctic, in which the kinship system is really an all-purpose organization used in various ways to solve legal, political, social, hunting, and other problems. Until about 8000 B.C. all of our ancestors lived in such cultures. After that date, people in several parts of the world began to experiment with animals and plants and eventually became stock breeders and cultivators. The development of a secure form of agriculture was usually a process that took two to three thousand years. It led to settled life in villages with larger social groups. It also laid the economic basis for civilization.

Between 5000 and 1200 B.C., six world areas produced new forms of culture that we call civilizations. In their native zones, each of these new cultures was different from anything that had gone before, and yet they were each in-place developments, owing none of their new sophistication to outside cultures. They superseded and incorporated into themselves the preceding village societies, which were characterized by consensual governance, limited numbers of people, relatively low levels of violence, relatively incoherent folk beliefs about the universe, and limited economic exchanges of basic commodities and manufactures. The new civilized ways of life meant that economic exchange became specialized, with formal markets handling much of the activity. Religion developed along the lines of theologies, that is, coherent systems of belief. Early forms of the state developed systems of decision that became centralized and exclusive, with small inner groups taking control of relatively rationalized administrative organizations. Villages, towns, and hamlets became beholden to a new form of community, the city. Cities assumed the control and integration functions of the new political, economic, religious, and social systems. All cultural forms eventually became hierarchically organized. Class and caste societies based on political and religious status became the norm, replacing the older ranked societies of farming villages. To put it more succinctly, but perhaps less comprehensibly, the new complex cultures reorganized all major cultural institutions (economics, social structure, politics, religion) along hierarchical lines.

These revolutionary developments took place in only six restricted areas of the world: the Middle East, Egypt, the Indus Valley, and China in the Old World and Mesoamerica and the Andean areas of the New World. The New World areas were separated from the Old World cultures by the vast Pacific and Atlantic oceans, and there is no good evidence of any interaction.

Old World Pristine Civilizations

The Middle East

The Middle Eastern culture sphere is very large (see Map 1.1); consideration of the Middle East usually excludes Egypt because of the latter's apparently unique and independent development of high culture. That leaves a geographic area of approximately 1,547,000 km² (ca. 597,000 mi²) that runs north to south from the Black Sea to the Persian Gulf and

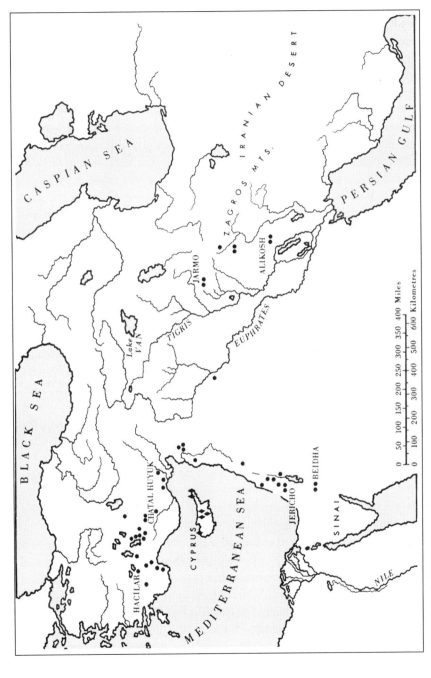

MAP 1.1   Middle East cultures

east to west from the interior deserts of Iran to the Mediterranean. The great twin rivers of the Euphrates on the west and the Tigris on the east make up the central drainage basin, which is rimmed with mountains on the north, east, and west and by deserts on the south. The other major zone, the great peninsula occupied by present-day Turkey, is characterized by mountains, plateaus, and rivers that drain into the surrounding seas. The coastal shelf of the Levant runs from present-day Lebanon to the Gaza area, and the edge of the Mediterranean is paralleled by mountain ranges with small interior valleys such as the Bekka and the Jordan.

This geographic diversity, combined with an area large enough to promote cultural differences through isolation, appears to be a sufficient characteristic of most of the areas of early civilizations. The apparent necessary factor was that human cultures in the area came into ever more frequent contact and intense interaction. In the Middle East this interaction began through trade in both basic and even frivolous commodities, such as obsidian, salt, and seashell jewelry in the Upper Palaeolithic (ca. twenty thousand years ago). By the time of the proliferation of farming villages and population growth (ca. 6500 B.C.), people had firmed up trade networks, which were woven around permanent settlements and carried an ever-increasing array of commodities and manufactures. Hybridization improved plants and animals; these hybrids were added to local inventories where they had not been present before. The technological advances, inventions, and goods that were continually passed through webs of interchange included copper and bronze technologies, infinite varieties of pottery, ideas about building (domes, buttresses, standardized floorplans, and so on), and other matters such as the proper arrangements of a well-ordered society. By 6500 B.C. most people in the Middle East lived in single-story houses of mud brick (adobe) that were clustered together into small farming villages. However, two sites of the Neolithic period (ca. 9000–5000 B.C.) were unusual and provide a startling look at possible new cultural developments (Mellaart 1975).

Jericho, as it existed in the Jordan Valley of the Holy Land at about 7800 B.C., was a community of perhaps fifteen hundred people. They had built their houses about the springs that are still one of the major attractions of the site (Kenyon 1957). These houses were round and had domed roofs, a rather imaginative use of physical principles for the time. Further, the community was surrounded by a formidable wall that still is about 3.3 m (11 feet) high and included features such as towers with interior staircases at least 7 m (23 feet) in height. Kathleen Kenyon, the excavator of

Jericho, had only a glimpse of these earliest levels of the site, given the fact that they lie under 23 m (75 feet) or so of later debris. At about 7000 B.C. the inhabitants of Jericho changed the shape of their houses to the kind of two-room *megaron* plan that is the basis for the much-later Classical Greek houses and temples of about 400 B.C. They had rebuilt the fortifications and improved them with a dry ditch into the bedrock around the town. There are two major possibilities for investing such a great amount of energy and time in defenses. One is that the traditional Middle Eastern enmity between nomads and village dwellers already existed. There is strong evidence that some of the hunters and gatherers of 11,000 B.C. had chosen to herd animals and thereby keep their old nomadic way of life. (It should be noted that these early nomads were probably goat and sheep herders; camels and dromedaries were not domesticated until very late.) There is also the possibility that somewhere in the vicinity was an equally advanced town considered to be a menace by the inhabitants of Jericho. No such site has been reported to date, however.

Striking developments in religion are present in Jericho in the form of the famous human skulls with modeled stucco facial portraits. These items possibly represent the esteemed and deceased members of families being used in ancestor reverence. Small clay figurines of human females seem to represent a kind of fertility cult—an identification of human life cycles with natural cycles in general.

A considerable distance away, in southern Anatolia, was Chatal Huyuk, another innovative Neolithic community that was partly contemporary with Jericho (Mellaart 1967). Chatal Huyuk was a town of about 13 ha (32 acres) in extent that reached its peak at about 6400 B.C. The houses were built of adobe bricks with abutting walls; they lacked windows or doors but had access through clerestories in the roofs. This gave the town a spurious similarity to pueblos of groups in the southwestern United States. Inside the single-roomed houses, however, there is an astounding display of Neolithic art in the form of murals, modeled stucco reliefs, and other productions. Most of the art is dedicated to religious subjects and especially to the "mother goddess" and her consort. Again, without dwelling on detail, the Neolithic fertility cult is identified with the natural cycles of birth, life, death, and rebirth. The burial of women and children in the house benches and some mural evidence indicates a reverence for the dead and possibly something like ancestor commemoration. The mother goddess's characteristics at Chatal Huyuk are very similar to those of later Classic-era goddesses of the Mediterranean. Mellaart (1967) suggests that these similarities are not accidental and that somehow, and no doubt indirectly, these religious conceptions were transmitted over the millennia to later Classical periods with their descendant goddesses such as Artemis and Diana. These early and innovative towns were not the norm, however; that was established by the hundreds of smaller Neolithic villages. Neither were Jericho and Chatal Huyuk representatives of early civilization. There is no strong evidence of their heading or belonging to formal political, economic, or social systems.

By 5500 B.C. population growth had transformed the Middle Eastern landscapes from thinly occupied areas to zones in which villages were clearly in sight of one another and land scarcity was evident. By about 5300 B.C. the first settlements had been established in southern Mesopotamia, and by 5000 B.C. several walled towns existed in the southern valley. These communities show most of the features of cities, and their sustaining cultures are hierarchically organized. The transforming factors are disputed among specialists, but it does appear that population growth continued in irregular patterns. Economics and long-distance trade show many signs of becoming more complex. Indeed Wright and Johnson (1975) argue that trade was a major altering factor in producing civilization. The demands of living in a landscape devoid of most resources other than land and water forced the importation of a variety of commodities. The spaces involved between early towns and cities such as Eridu were such that considerable thought, energy, and investment were needed to establish regular caravans, warehouses, accounting systems, and other features of long-distance exchange. The establishment of irrigation systems made organizational demands. Warfare, ever an accelerator of cultural change, also seems to have hastened the process of change toward more elaborate institutions.

The culture of ancient Sumer (for that is what the southern valley became) is relatively well known. At first, the political systems apparently were diverse forms of city-states. These appear to have evolved from various forms of complex chiefdoms (Wright 1994) that had, in turn, possibly developed from the needs of trade. These early civilized communities had certain characteristics in common. They were all defended by walls. Defenses enclosed large public buildings that include the famous ziggurats (temple platforms), and what seem to have been large and many-roomed palace structures. Both temples and palaces were surrounded by auxiliary buildings, including kitchens, storerooms, and fairly humble residential rooms. These establishments were in turn surrounded by houses of fairly standardized plans that were used in later traditional Middle Eastern cultures. All buildings were made of adobe bricks; the more elaborate were decorated with colored stones, cones, glazed tiles (in a later period), murals, modeled stucco, and other embellishments. These cities were supported by farmers who operated irrigated, intensive farming systems in the countryside. Populations probably ranged from three to nine thousand, judging by the extent of urban areas and comparative material from preindustrial cities elsewhere. The economic base also included large amounts of traded materials, especially wool from flocks of sheep owned corporately by the temples or by individual farmers. Food and trade surpluses supported the corporate enterprises of temple and state.

In regard to the political systems, the archaeological evidence and much later textual information conflict to some degree. Based on Wooley's excavations at Ur (Wooley 1954), it appears that the institution of divine kingship was in place by 2500 B.C. Wooley found sixteen magnificent tombs at Ur in which a few people were buried in a sumptuous manner, accompanied by large numbers of servants, concubines, guards, oxen, musical instruments, and vessels and jewelry of gold, among other items. This practice, called retainer burial, is found when a divinely sanctioned monarch dies and requires that his status in life be maintained in death. In short, a divine ruler attempts to take it all with him (or her).

These and other finds imply a highly centralized, aristocratic political system, one sanctioned by religion. However, the picture from the limited texts from 3000 B.C. onward imply a system that is quite different. Some scholars claim that it was democratic (Kramer 1963). According to the standard interpretations of the cuneiform texts, Sumerian civilization was one of free men who met in a body to make decisions but who also deferred to certain temple and palace leaders. Given the despotic nature of slightly later cultures of the area and the archaeological data, this reconstructed system seems to be almost wholly unrealistic or limited in time and space to a few exceptional cities and states.

Whatever the political system (and it does appear to have become despotic sooner or later), certain administrative tools were developed that have come down to us. Writing is possibly the most important means of transmittal of information, both for immediate purposes and for posterity. Its origins are seen in the needs for a notation system that could handle accounts and other economic data. Later scribes experimented with the possibilities of the logographic (syllabic) cuneiform system and developed a fully fledged script capable of carrying an abstract message without the necessity of a memorized explanatory text. Complex art forms were also used to inspire awe, to communicate, and to beautify the urban scene. Technological progress and invention led to concepts and tools that are still in use. The 60-minute hour, 60-second minute, and 360-degree circle are examples of the cultural legacies coming down to us from the Sumerians, who used a base 60 mathematical system.

In spite of recurrent catastrophes and disasters, Middle Eastern civilizations went through an extraordinarily complex and long development that illustrates one of the great distinguishing characteristics of civilized cultures—their capacity for reformation and renewal. The Middle East went on in this way for thousands of years until the beginning of the eighth century A.D., the point at which A. L. Kroeber (1963) suggests that Islam swept the area as a purifying and simplifying movement. The great number of permutations and the lasting nature of cultural patterns within the area are undoubtedly due to the great numbers of people that eventually participated in these cultures. No matter how dire the disaster, some people were always left to start over and carry on the traditions, albeit in some new version. We will see that this also happened in the New World, where even with a population loss of 90 to 95 percent after the Spanish conquest, native cultural patterns have survived to the present day. However, these examples in Native American cultures are what might be considered the basic and least elaborate patterns, suitable to a village society rather than a civilization.

Egypt

The ancient Greek travel writer, Herodotus, first described Egypt as "the gift of the Nile," but that characterization must have been ancient even when he articulated it. From the traditional southern boundary—the first cataract of the Nile—north to the Mediterranean, Egypt is a long narrow land running between cliffs and deserts that bound it on east and west (see Map 1.2). Including the Nile delta and the Fayum overflow basin, arable land totals only about 34,000 km² (13,127 mi²). The extremes of the deserts are modified only by the Nile, which until recently flooded each year, not only depositing a renewing layer of soil but also rinsing away salts harmful to domesticated plants.

Agricultural development of the Nile and the adjacent Fayum overflow basin began perhaps as early as 6000 B.C. and possibly independently of such development in the adjacent Middle East. Small villages of farmers established themselves on the edges of the periodically flooded zones of

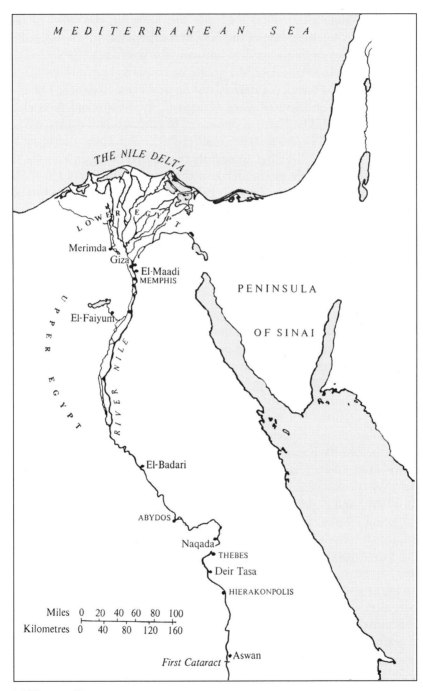

MAP 1.2   Egypt

the Nile. From about 6000 B.C. onward, however, the band of rain-watered land on either side of the Nile in southern Egypt shrank, a situation that drove cattle pastoralists in upon the river (Bard 1994:267). At first there was an abundance of animals and birds to hunt, which filled in the diet of wheat bread, vegetables, and domesticated livestock. The question is still hotly disputed as to whether Egypt owes much—or anything—to the Middle East for donations of domesticated plants and animals. By 3500 B.C., a series of small political and economic units had appeared along the Nile that apparently segmented the river from the first cataract in the south to the delta in the north (Hoffman 1979; Bard 1994). Two groups of Predynastic cultures can be distinguished by that date, corresponding to the two major parts of the great river. These culturally distinct areas differed in material culture as well as in ideology. Population growth and development of state and temple leadership groups apparently led to the competitive atmosphere of the next period. By 3300 B.C., military force was being used to conquer and consolidate previously independent principalities. Walled towns are shown on pieces of art from this Late Predynastic period, together with symbolic scenes of battle, siege, and beheaded enemies. A number of early rulers were probably involved in this, but the names of only a half dozen have come down to us in written (hieroglyphic) form.

By about 3050 B.C., Egypt had been politically consolidated into a single centralized state. The process of how this came about is debated among specialists, but it appears that the southern kingdom expanded into the north and especially over the delta. The consolidating conquests noted before have traditionally been interpreted as campaigns against towns in the delta (Bard 1994:282). The former division into two major parts was preserved in the title of the pharaohs, who were kings of Upper (northern) and Lower (southern) Egypt. Kings "Scorpion," Narmer (Catfish), and Menes were apparently the rulers of Upper Egypt who finally unified the whole land (Aldred 1965:42–52). Small towns and large temple centers had functioned as the administrative and regional market centers for the segments of the Nile. These units survived into the Dynastic period as *nomes*, which were subordinate to the pharaoh's ministers in the bureaucratic hierarchy.

An ideology that included a religious pattern placed the ruler at the top of society as a divine king. The preparation for the afterlife became an obsessive part of Egyptian culture down to the lowest classes. Egyptian society was structured about the castelike aristocracy below the pharaoh and was highly specialized into occupations. The whole structure rested on the patient and overworked farmers who produced the huge amounts of grain and other resources needed to sustain it. Most of these people lived in the kinds of villages that existed in the Predynastic period and that still exist today in parts of Egypt. Of all the Old World civilizations, the Egyptian was probably the most conservative. It was only when the Romans came to rule that some changes took place, and these appear not to have been fundamental. Alexander the Great, after all, had previously been incorporated into Egyptian theology as yet another god-king. Revolutionary changes only occurred in the eighth century A.D. when the more egalitarian ideology of Islam swept the old order from the palaces, and even then the peasantry continued to follow its age-old lifestyle (Kroeber 1963).

China

The ecologically complex area occupied by ancient Chinese culture is also geographically vast, the largest of the Old World early civilizations (see Map 1.3). However, the heartland of complex development is likely less than half of the traditional area of China, or about 3,885,000 km^2 (1.5 million mi^2). This core area is centered on the two great east-west river systems: the Huang-ho (Yellow River) in the north and the Yangtze in the south. Huge amounts of work by Chinese archaeologists in both the early and late twentieth century deplorably are mostly inaccessible to Western scholars who do not read Chinese. Fortunately, Professor Kwang-chih Chang has done an immense service by his periodic and increasingly valuable syntheses of the prehistory of that ancient land. I have depended nearly wholly on the fourth edition of his work (Chang 1986) as well as on personal communications (1994).

The Chinese cultivated various crops, such as roots and tubers in the southern coastal zones and millets and rice in the interior river valleys, by 5500 B.C. (Chang 1986:102, 107). Pigs were probably domesticated by 6400 B.C. in southern China. In spite of the size and complexity of the country, there was a fairly rapid spread of village life and an increasing trend to homogeneity of culture in the Neolithic. This period was one of long duration (6500 to 2000 B.C.), with many regional variants. An early kind of Neolithic culture has only recently been found, of which the P'ei-li-kang is well known and appears ancestral to the next phase.

The best-known and one of the most widespread of the Neolithic cultures is the Yang Shao culture (5000–3000 B.C.), which centered on the

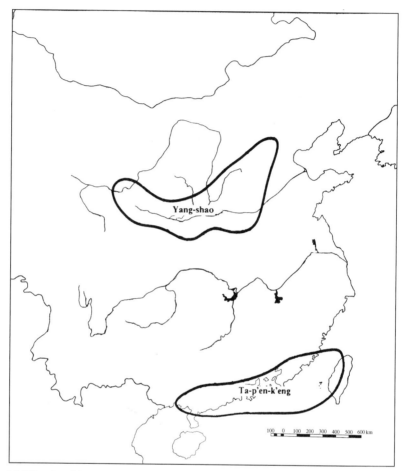

MAP 1.3   China

Huang-ho River. Dogs and pigs were the most important domesticated animals, although cattle, goats, and sheep were present. Silkworms were early cared for, and by implication, silk cloth was manufactured. Pan-p'o, located on a major tributary of the Huang-ho, the Wei-shui River, is one of the best-preserved villages for this period. The community was made up of a variety of houses covering an area of approximately 50,000 m^2 (12 + acres). Permanent facilities included a huge communal structure in the center of the village together with a cemetery, animal pens, pottery kilns, and a storage pit. Another village at Chiang-chai has houses grouped in a way that strongly suggests the presence of lineages and clans, the kinship units that were the basis of later traditional Chinese society. All evidence is that these villages were self-sufficient communities and that they also derived a great deal of food from hunting and gathering (Chang 1986:93, 114). The ingenious villagers produced beautifully painted pottery in the kilns and made and used great numbers of different tools. Potters' marks are a kind of notation that might be ancestral to writing.

The pattern of cultivation appears to have been slash and burn, a shifting system requiring a village to change location periodically. In the north the principal grain was the foxtail millet. In the south, a Neolithic variant called the Ta p'en-k'eng culture was likely the first in China to cultivate rice, a plant native to monsoon Asia. Analysis of the skeletons from one village cemetery indicates that about 19 percent of the population died before the age of twenty and that about 50 percent had died before the age of fifty (Chang 1986:121).

At about 3200 B.C. widespread transformations took place in the three principal zones of Neolithic China: the south coast, the Yangtze, and the Huang-ho. These changes led to the appearance of a cultural group known as the Lung-shanoid cultures, which were astonishingly similar in spite of the large area over which they were spread (Chang 1986:241). The early phase of change was one resulting in permanently located villages and egalitarian societies. The late phase of transformation led to warlike and ranked societies (Chang 1986:244).

Changes in this late Neolithic set of cultures were profound, and only a few can be mentioned here. An expansion to the east of the farming cultures was accompanied by a great increase in the herding of cattle and sheep. "The successful planting of rice and the use of a broader range of food resources undoubtedly gave these farmers a greater ability to adapt to a greater variety of environments in central and south China" (Chang 1977:172). Occupational specializations were tied to technological developments such as the use of the potter's wheel. Handsome, lustrous black pottery was produced as well as carved jade items using symbols that appear ancestral to historical motifs. Walled towns indicate a lack of security in the countryside and an increase in warfare. Certain regional cultures show great disparity in burial practices, with some people buried very simply and others with great ceremony and many offerings. The implication of ranked society is important, for it means that eventual class differences were probably based in these earlier times. The emergence of civilized life as a new form of culture took place at about 2100 B.C. with the appear-

ance of what may be Hsia dynasty material (2100–1800 B.C.). Although
the center of the development appears to have been in the present-day
area of Honan (central China), there were significant contributions from
other zones. In fact, the Hsia dynasty probably preceded the Shang as the
founders of the earliest state, but there is still some debate about this matter (Chang 1986:314–316).

The site of Erh-li-t'ou has given its name to the archaeological culture
of the Hsia period. Very early palace structures have been defined and
have many of the same features as later historical residences of the aristocracy (Chang 1986:310–311). Bronze items such as bells and wine servers
were also found. Small houses for lower-class people found near the
palaces are rectangular in plan and had timber framework. Well-furnished
burials of the upper classes and impoverished graves of the commoners
were found, with additional indications of human sacrifice (Chang
1986:312–314). Warfare increased and the Hsia were eventually conquered by the leaders of the Shang dynasty, who gained a military edge by
the extensive use of war chariots. The Shang began their six-hundred-year
domination of China with their first capital city, Po, which may be an archaeological site located in Yen-shih. The somewhat later Shang site of
Cheng-chou, under the present-day city of the same name, is possibly the
former capital city of Ao. The city was defended by a massive rammed-
earth structure enclosing an area of 3.2 km² (ca. 1.2 mi²). It is estimated
that such a structure would have taken ten thousand men eighteen years
to build. Such an accomplishment is evidence of a truly centralized political and economic control. Bronze foundries, residential remains, and various workshops were found outside the walls. Bronze workers enjoyed a
better standard of living than commoners.

The final capital of the Shang is known to have been called Yin and is
identified with the great site of An-yang. Seventeen sites are actually
known from this zone, and they are scattered over an area of 24 km² (ca.
9.2 mi²). The structures of An-yang include palace buildings constructed
and occupied possibly for the 273 years mentioned in literary sources. At
Hsiao-t'un site, palaces were surrounded by humble houses, workshops,
and tombs. North of the Huan River there is an aristocratic cemetery as
well as "many thousand sacrificial burials" (An Chih-min et al., in Chang
1986:320–322). Huge numbers of inscribed oracle bones found in the
An-yang sites form an invaluable body of written texts that appear to be
only the tip of an iceberg of records that once included numberless administrative communications. Eleven large tombs were found that coin-

cide with the eleven rulers mentioned in the later histories. All are deep within the earth, and each was built at the cost of at least seven thousand working days. A wooden coffin was placed in the central pit, and many sacrificial burials accompanied the main occupant. Huge numbers of artifacts of various materials and often of exquisite workmanship have been found, including the highly prized Shang bronzes. From later literary sources it is known that the rulers considered themselves of divine origin. This seems confirmed by the retainer burials. An aristocracy was formed by the royal lineages, who were strongly patrilineal. Shoulder bones of certain animals had been fire cracked and marked with symbols, a practice known as scapulimancy. These are the famous oracle bones that have their origins in the Lung-shan cultures and were one of the means by which the ancestors were contacted. Ancestor worship was institutionalized, also a Neolithic cultural inheritance. Religion and ritual were highly developed and had most of the later features of Chinese ideological life. Ancestral temples were oriented to the four directions, and the gods were also parceled out in this manner. Gods and goddesses of various natural kinds (sun, moon, earth, and so on) were also ruled over by a supreme deity. Royalty were able to contact the ancestors and the gods easily. The great art of the Shang was largely tied to religious conceptions, which led to persistent symmetry in art and in ritual and historical cycles.

Craftsmen were of elevated status in Shang times but were not aristocratic. The existence of potters, bronze makers, carpenters, chariot makers, tailors, armorers, and many other occupations can be inferred from as well as being mentioned in the texts. Farmers raised millets, rice, and wheat, with the first two yielding two crops a year, probably through use of irrigation. Hemp and silkworms were raised for cloth. Pigs, dogs, cattle, water buffalo, sheep, horses, and chickens were all raised.

The Shang dynasty was followed by the Chou and then by the Warring States period, by the end of which China was finally unified in 221 B.C. By the time of the Hsia and beginning of the Shang, however, Chinese civilization had assumed the general characteristics of early complex societies as well as the distinctive features that set it apart for the next four thousand years.

The Harrapan Civilization of the Indus Valley

The Harrapan civilization occupied a great river system, the Indus and its tributaries, and spread east along the coast to the area of present-day

Bombay. The civilization covered an expanse of perhaps 80,000 km^2 (30,888 mi^2) (see Map 1.4).

Four very large cities are known, two of which have been explored: Mohenjo-daro in the central Indus zone and Harrapa in the upper tributary region. More than a thousand smaller towns and sites are known, although excavations have lagged behind survey work.

The earliest village cultures in the Indus Valley are not obviously ancestral to the Harrapan civilization, and a suitable origin culture is yet to be found. Fairservice (1971, 1991) considers the villages of the Baluchistan valleys to have been the probable origin areas for the Indus populations and says that those cultures ultimately derived from those of Neolithic Iran. Moving from these zones into the lower and much hotter valley floor would have required some major adjustments. The valley has its advantages, nonetheless, and the flow of the Indus is twice that of the Nile. It is certain that by about 3000 B.C. residents of agricultural villages along the river cultivated wheat, barley, and field peas and probably dates and melons. Irrigation would have been necessary, given the relatively slight rainfall of the area. This may have led to the eventual collapse of the civilization: Raikes (1964) and Dales (1966) have suggested that the area is subject to gradual geological uplift and that this may have affected irrigation systems. Salinization, too, may have been an eventual problem. However, by 2500 B.C. it seems that some of the earliest urban efforts were made at Mohenjo-daro. What spurred this surge toward a new form of society is not clear, but it may have been that religious and economic leadership had passed into the hands of a small group. Fairservice (1991) certainly considers that this is a probable scenario. This process is the sort of thing that Colin Renfrew argues (in Edey 1975:28) happened much later in the eastern Mediterranean when "bullies or smooth talkers" assumed control of the grape (wine) and olive trade. With the resultant surpluses, it was possible to expand power over the neighboring countryside and thus to support a new and larger form of community. In the Harrapan case, however, it appears that the commodities in question were cattle, goats, and sheep. Further, it appears that they were moved from lowlands to highlands and back again in an annual cycle attuned to the weather, a form of life known as transhumance (Fairservice 1991).

The new cities provided more security and luxurious living for the elite and perhaps were better for the commoners who supported the elite. Certainly the Mohenjo-daro data indicate a surprisingly high standard of living for nearly all classes. However, the villages around the cities were scat-

MAP 1.4   India

tered widely and evidently continued to spread through space as time went on. The reasons for this geographical spread are best stated in Fairservice's own words: "If, as seems likely, wealth was counted in number-of-cattle, the demand for grazing land, fodder and secure sources of water would have threatened agriculture. The answer was to move to new areas where a balance might be achieved, at least momentarily" (Fairservice 1991:112). He goes on to explain that such expansion would weaken the redistribution system and tribute collecting controlled by the elite, therefore leading to an eventual collapse of the Harrapan system and abandonment of the centers. The majority of Harrapan sites were occupied for less than two hundred years.

Both of the major cities, Mohenjo-daro and Harrapa, reflect intensive and rational urban planning. The entire city of Mohenjo-daro apparently was built on a gigantic brick platform to raise it above the flood waters, and thus was a truly planned center. Central citadels made of baked brick dominate both cities; Wheeler (1966:18) points out that they contain the equivalent of modern state banks in the form of large granaries. At Mohenjo-daro, the best-excavated of the two sites, there is also a Great Bath that appears to anticipate the ritual baths of historic and modern India. Large halls with roofs supported by pillars occur as well. Outside the citadel walls, the city proper was highly rectified in its plan, with major avenues 13.7 m (45 feet) wide and lined with shops as well as smaller lanes that gave access to commoner housing. City blocks with dozens of baked brick houses exhibited standardization of features if not planning. Most houses are made up of rooms clustered about interior courtyards with stairs leading to the formerly intact roofs or second stories. Privies are common and were attached to drains and water chutes that, in turn, led to major sewers under the streets. Wells and occasional baths occur as well.

Lothal is a city near the seacoast but away from the Indus that has features that led its excavator, S. R. Rao, to construe it as a seaport. However, this interpretation has been severely criticized, and it may be that what appears to be a mooring area complete with docks and bollards is really a very large version of the traditional Indian tank-bath. In any case, Lothal has most of the characteristic features of Harrapan cities and towns: mud brick buildings, rectilinear structures, urban layout, and reasonably commodious and comfortable residences.

Specializations in crafts are shown by the high quality pottery turned out by efficient mass production, even though the ceramic decoration is unimpressive. Seals were carved mainly in steatite and were used to impress clay bosses on bales and other commodity packaging. They appear to represent personal names but also carry a number of examples of script. Therefore, Indus writing appears to have been stimulated in part by the needs of commerce, although the script has yet to be deciphered. Over four hundred individual signs are known, which suggests to specialists that the script is syllabic (Fairservice 1971:278).

There are dozens of villages and small towns in the countryside, and with more information these may prove to form a settlement hierarchy, that would, in turn, reflect various administrative levels. There is little doubt that the cities of the Indus were the hearts of ancient states and that huge amounts of manpower and wealth were available to create the cities.

Particularly impressive is the overwhelming evidence of an almost military discipline in this culture reflected in the rigorous and standardized planning of many structures and in the massive public works. In spite of much recent work, this is the least known and most enigmatic of all the Old World civilizations, although there are clear cultural features that link the Harrapans to the historic Indian cultures.

Summary and Discussion

A great archaeologist viewing the course of development of Old World civilizations thought that he saw a number of common elements. He listed ten of these as inevitable components of early cities and, therefore, early civilizations (Childe 1950). Although Childe's list is now somewhat outdated, it was on the right track. Looking at all the Old World early complex cultures, there always seem to be cities, whether large or small, that performed similar functions. They were the administrative, economic, religious, and social centers for their societies. In the parlance of the 1960s, ancient cities were where the action was. It has been argued that Egypt had no true cities until very late. Technically this may be so, but early towns did exist, and at least one was fortified. The point is that the functions of civilized life were performed by relatively small and elite groups of people in preindustrial times as well as in ancient periods. Sometimes these groups clustered around palaces, as in Late Bronze Age Crete (Minoan civilization), and many times they aggregated together with commoners into larger settlements we can call cities, characteristic of the Middle East, China, and the Indus.

In our secularized age, it is important to remember how important religion was as an integrating mechanism and a motivating force. Religious leadership was not necessarily divorced from political office, and often the two were tied together. Slaves did not build the pyramids in Egypt, nor the great Maya temples in the New World. Religious beliefs motivated people in both cases, just as in the Middle Ages of Europe great numbers of people labored to the glory of God on cathedrals. In all of the Old World complex cultures, religion appears to have been an early and crucial factor in drawing people together for various communal projects. The temple centers of Egypt and the Middle East became economic powers in their own rights, and their managers began to wield unusual influence. All early political leaders in early civilizations seem to have had religious confirmation. Divine kingship appeared in Egypt, the Middle East, and

China and may have been present in the Indus area. Early civilizations of the New World also had this institution, although, as in the Old World, political leadership gradually became secularized through time.

A number of other elements characterize early civilizations. Of these, writing, or a system of notation, seems to be universal. The need for an accounting system to keep track of taxes, tribute, income, expenses, and all the additional data that go with the numbers led to writing in the Middle East and perhaps in Egypt. Propaganda and religious needs also were important in the origins of Egyptian writing. In China, it was divination, especially on the state level or for the benefit of the rulers, that led to writing. In all cases worldwide, with one exception, once notation was invented it eventually grew to be a writing system capable of handling abstract messages. The exception is the culture of the Incas, which I will discuss later.

State-level systems, more or less hierarchically organized, all occur in early complex cultures. Efficiency of administration, centralized control, elite class security, oligarchic desire for retention of power, and other motivations were all involved in state development.

One of the major differences between Old and New World civilizations lies in their technological developments. Essentially, the Old World cultures continued their adoption of inventions, techniques, mechanics, and systematic accumulation of knowledge. In some cases and periods, technology was deliberately or inadvertently halted, but this was never a complete stasis and development eventually recovered. In the New World, technology was much less important and essentially Stone Age. In Egypt, technological innovation in floodplain (recessional) agriculture meant that elements of plane geometry used for land survey were developed. In China and elsewhere, much calculation and empirical knowledge were involved in agricultural terracing, wet rice paddy farming, large-scale irrigation canal systems, and other elements. In all of the Old World, surpluses in food, commodities, and manufactured items led to trade—first local, then regional, and later long distance. Ancient economic systems always (and even today) outstripped political systems in their complexity and extent. In an evolutionary sense, therefore, economic systems seem to nearly always precede political control.

Militarism appeared early in the Old World as an accelerator of the development of ever more complexity. Large-scale, well-organized warfare, lamentable as it may be, seems to have been an inevitable development along with other new elements in early civilized cultures. Fortifications, specialized classes of soldiers, and tactical and technological develop-ments all interacted with other cultural institutions.

Having gained something of a global and comparative perspective on the nature of the earliest civilizations in the Old World, we can now turn to the major subject of this book: the native civilizations of the New World.

2

Mesoamerica:
Origins and Early Civilizations

The culture area of Mesoamerica makes up a little over 1 million km² (397,000 mi²) in what are now the countries of Guatemala, Mexico, Belize, El Salvador, and eastern Honduras (see Map 2.1). It is an area of striking ecological diversity created by mountainous terrain, coastal plains, and a limestone platform (Yucatan) situated in tropical and subtropical latitudes. Volcanic eruptions are common, as are earthquakes, hurricanes, and less drastic modifications of the landscape. Altitude, rainfall, and soil differences create innumerable regional variants. As noted elsewhere (Adams 1991:15), "compressed ecological diversity" is a succinct way of characterizing the area.

Mesoamerica was a vast area of cultural diversity but one bound together by a set of common technologies, cultural institutions, and especially world views. Thus, even though as many as thirty regional civilizations came and went, all participated in the great traditions of the area. Fundamental to all of these regional blossomings was a set of agricultural systems that sooner or later achieved very intense forms. Swamp drainage, land reclamation, canal irrigation, and hillside terracing are examples of the food production methods that sustained millions and supported cities with their elites and craftsmen.

Mixed classes and caste societies with aristocratic rulers and administrators were organized into city- and regional states, with occasional empires appearing. The village was first and always the fundamental social and political unit; early regional centers gave way to large regional centers and then to cities and towns. Long-distance trade, religious pilgrimages, political alliances, and warfare tied the regions together and assured that

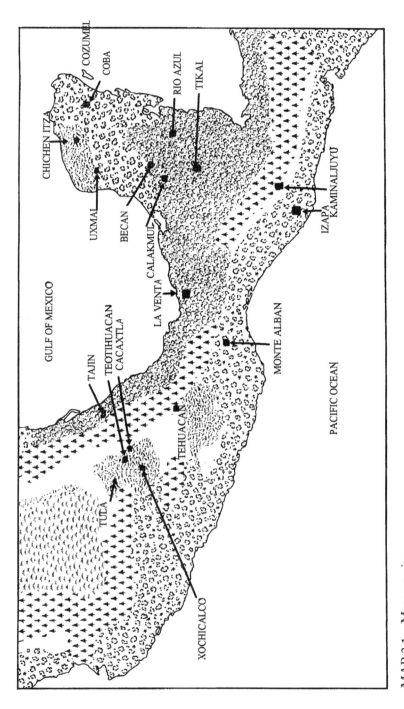

MAP 2.1 Mesoamerica

most innovations were widely and rapidly spread. Art and script in various media were used for propaganda, historical, and administrative purposes.

Technology depended heavily on stone tools and lacked the wheel, draft animals, or many mechanical devices. Metals were used only late and then largely for ornamental purposes. Transportation was by water where possible and by human porter where necessary. Fortunately, much of Mesoamerica was accessible from its coasts, lagoons, rivers, and lakes. Architecture was of cut stone, high quality lime mortar, and plaster supplemented by timber. These materials were used to build cities, which were often linked by stone-paved roads and causeways as well as by water. The small city-state was the basic unit that was often combined into larger political systems.

A fatalistic ethos permeated Mesoamerican religions and world views. Gods were capricious and often malignant. Cosmic destruction had occurred before the present world. Human sacrifice was the ultimate offering to stave off the ever-present threat of destruction or disaster, but other sacrifices were also required. Calendars and mathematics regulated the cycles of ritual, life, and even war. Rulers pursued divinely sanctioned wars as well as more mundanely inspired conflicts, and fortifications littered the landscape. The origins of these societies lie deep in the past and to understand them we must search in the earliest hunter-gatherer and farming-village cultures. These simpler societies ultimately were the source of many of the later complex traits.

Laying the Basis for Civilization: 7000–1500 B.C.

The basic human concerns of getting enough to eat, sheltering from the weather, and clothing oneself against the elements were all problems that had long since been solved in the Palaeolithic of the Old World. Northeastern Siberia and Alaska formed a continuous land bridge over which the first immigrants traveled into the New World. They carried Old World cultural patterns with them as well as a basic stone tool kit and the even more valuable knowledge of how to hunt and prepare animals and plants for eating. These imported skills, information, and technology accompanied the first people into Mesoamerica as well as into the rest of the New World. That was a world of ice and snow in the northern latitudes, although farther south it was mostly a climate of heavier rainfall and cooler climate than at present.

Recent, convincing evidence from Alaska and Canada makes it likely that humans came into the New World later than was previously thought to be the case, with the earliest immigrants coming through a newly hospitable land bridge about 12,000 B.C. (Hoffecker et al. 1993). Although the complex debate over this matter is still not fully resolved, in the opinion of this professional the weight of the evidence is on the side of late entry. About 7000 B.C. changes in climate due to the retreat and melting of the glaciers resulted in fewer animals to hunt and the extinction of many larger species such as the giant forms of elephants, beavers, sloths, and bison. A gradual shift to intensive collecting of plants and the hunting of smaller animals took place over many generations. At the same time a considerable amount of experimentation was going on with cultivation of plants. The New World in general and Mesoamerica in particular were impoverished in the numbers of animal species left after the Ice Age extinctions. Horses died out completely, and it is thought that perhaps human hunting had something to do with their extinction and that of other species. The ancestral forms of modern cattle, pigs, goats, and sheep were not present in the New World, an absence that led to problems in gaining sufficient animal protein in later diets. Therefore, the problem that confronted the New World hunters and gatherers at about 7000 B.C. was how to build up a set of domesticated plants sufficient to provide large amounts of food and a well-balanced diet.

Various archaeological projects over the past fifty years have documented the gradual transitions in different regions as people moved from nomadic but intensive exploitation of wild foods to settled cultivation of domesticated plants. R. S. MacNeish's work has ranged from the tropical lowlands of Belize to semiarid highlands of northeastern Mexico (MacNeish 1992). He has exploited many dry cave sites in which plant parts were preserved along with the ancient tools for gathering and processing them. This difficult work has produced evidence that demonstrates several features of the transitional period from hunting-gathering to agriculture. One is gradualism in the buildup toward village agricultural life. In no case was there a great leap forward or a rapid transition. Second, each region had its own inventory of native plants that varied slightly or greatly from that of other zones. Therefore, the first steps toward domestication of plants were accompanied by regional trading of plants. By this means selection of desirable traits and hybridization were accelerated. Eventually, each region of Mesoamerica emerged with a large set of native and imported plants that were suitable to its altitude, rainfall, and soils. Viable combinations of food plants were achieved in some precocious zones by 2000 B.C. and in most regions by about 1500 B.C.

Note that people's diets were composed almost entirely of vegetables, fruits, nuts, and berries, with very little coming from animals. The turkey and a native form of dog are the exceptions. Deer were tamed in some zones, and probably peccaries (javelinas) as well. Still, there was relatively little animal protein in Mesoamerican diets compared to that available to Old World cultures. Tropical and temperate zones traded products peculiar to each—cacao from the lowlands and avocados from the highlands, for example. If something could not be grown regionally, then it was available through commerce. Domestication of the major North American grain plant, corn *(Zea maize)*, was not achieved until relatively late, about 3000 B.C., and even then it was an unimproved variety good only for chewing for the juices. By 1600 B.C. improved and more productive varieties had been developed and adapted to nearly all Mesoamerican climates.

Pottery is a useful item, but only for sedentary people. In a nomadic way of life, leather bags, net bags, and basketry are lighter and more portable. Cooking in such containers, however, requires the use of a technique known as "stone-boiling." In this process heated stones are held with tongs and swirled in water or food. The first pottery in the New World was probably invented by people living on the Caribbean coast of Colombia about 3100 B.C., and it is possible that the idea spread slowly north. Pottery in Mesoamerica itself was invented or imported (it is not certain which) about 2200 B.C. In any case, by about 1600 B.C., nearly all Mesoamerican village cultures had adopted it. An average household in ethnographic cultures possesses from ten to fifteen pots at any given time. Several are for water carrying and storage, some are for food preparation and cooking, and still others are for food service. A few may be dedicated to ritual and aesthetics; specific examples are incense burners and flower vases. Ceramics are easily manufactured with natural materials available nearly everywhere and therefore were largely a home craft until very elaborately decorated pottery appeared as status items.

In fact, the first integrative process that pulled early human cultures together into large groups was the need for trade of commodities. Obsidian for stone tools, a multitude of plants, and salt were among the early and constant items of exchange. Small local centers grew up that were really large villages and that probably held periodic markets. By 1600 B.C. this growth had produced a hierarchy of settlements in some regions mainly based on size: hamlets, villages, and local centers. Because of the supposed need for management in such a situation, it is theorized that these new larger communities were run by leaders similar to those we call "chiefs" in modern Melanesia. However, in these early times, it is also possible that many other variants of management mechanisms were available. Councils of family heads, village elders, lineage leaders, or groups of women who had cornered market activities as in present-day Nigeria and Liberia are among the possibilities. In fact, it would be surprising if this period were not one of social experimentation.

Specialization in village economies appeared early in some zones such as the Valley of Mexico and likely elsewhere as well. By about 1200 B.C., in a few regions, new forms of society had appeared that were probably minor chiefdoms dominated by a single individual or a small group. Individuals of high status were buried with more elaborate grave offerings than those of their contemporaries. Certain groups seem to have accumulated wealth and power and to have reinforced these elements with religious sanctions. Two major deities are apparently reflected in the decorations of Early Preclassic ceramics of Mesoamerica. One god was a sort of crocodile that represented the earth's surface (the later Aztecs believed that the earth was a crocodile floating in the primordial sea). Another god was a sharklike fish that represented the watery underworld. A third god appeared about 900 B.C. in the form of a serpent; this one appears to have been adopted or developed by ruling groups as their special symbol (Grove 1992:161). These elaborate ceramics were found in a few special graves that presumably represent the leadership of these early chiefdoms. These ideas about the universe seem to have been very persuasive and widely accepted, although we cannot reconstruct the details. The motifs and the ideas they represented spread through many of the village cultures of the period. They were also expanded, combined, and manipulated in new ways by a culture that represents the earliest civilization in Mesoamerica—the Olmec.

The Olmec of the Gulf Coast

A great deal of work in the past forty years has shown that, although precocious, the Olmec were not the "mother culture" of Mesoamerica as was once thought (cf. Coe 1968:41–71). Conversely, David Grove (1981, 1992) concludes that Olmec culture essentially evolved in place on the Gulf Coast and therefore was not itself the result of donations of high culture from elsewhere. Small villages dating from 1750 to 1150 B.C. have been found in the La Venta and San Lorenzo zones (Rust and Sharer

1988; Coe and Diehl 1980). These communities are unremarkable in their physical features and look like most farming communities of the period. A major change came about after 1350 B.C. at San Lorenzo, where a hilltop location in the midst of swamps was expanded into a major artificial plateau requiring perhaps 2.13 million cubic meters (2.78 million cubic yards) of fill. Smaller platforms sat atop this gigantic base. Perishable buildings, possibly political and ritual in function, occupied the summits of the smaller platforms. The size of this first building project implies much more than a few small villages banding together. Leadership of a new order, populations of much larger sizes, perhaps of tens of thousands, and at least a vision of a new kind of religious center pushed these endeavors. Political ambitions and competition probably were operative factors as well. From 1250 B.C. forward, Olmec culture began to assume its special shape with the additional appearance of stone sculpture, hollow white-slipped pottery dolls, and greenstone jewelry (Grove 1981).

Although it is now accepted as true that the Olmec were not nearly as unique as they once appeared to be, neither were they simply "one of the gang" compared to other cultures of the area. Considering the order of magnitude of their achievements—building, great numbers of sophisticated sculptures, distribution of large-scale sculpture, long-distance trade contacts, the invention of parabolic mirrors, and exquisite greenstone jewelry—one must conclude that there was also a qualitative difference. The linkage of thresholds of scale with qualitative differences harks back to Georg Simmel's sociological work that showed that changes in internal sophistication were brought about by changes in size (Simmel 1950: 105–117). In terms of the theoretical framework laid out in Chapter 1, it appears that the Olmec had proceeded further and faster in their reorganization of cultural institutions than had their contemporaries. Although the Olmec held this edge for some time, they began to lose it when more advanced societies appeared at about 400 B.C. Meanwhile, Olmec leaders, whether despotic or oligarchic, managed to dominate their homeland, to extend their trade routes to far-flung parts of Mesoamerica, and to bring "foreigners" to the great Gulf Coast centers.

The long centuries of cultural domination must have seen a considerable internal development and political history. However, we know relatively little of that detail at the moment. Four very large centers are known: La Venta, San Lorenzo, Tres Zapotes, and Laguna de los Cerros. The first two have been excavated to some degree and are relatively well mapped (see Figure 2.1). The other two are mostly unknown except for

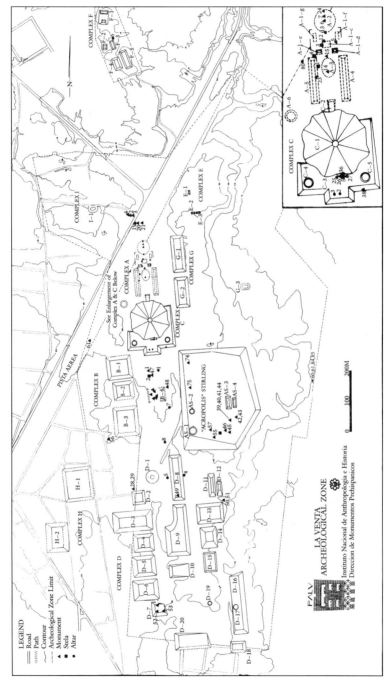

FIGURE 2.1   Site plan of the Olmec center of La Venta, Tabasco, Mexico. (Courtesy of Rebecca Gonzalez Lauck and INAH.)

preliminary mapping and a little test excavation. Therefore the following political reconstruction is tentative.

It has been suggested that the centers were the capitals of state-level polities and that they succeeded one another in some historical process not yet understood. There is some evidence that San Lorenzo was the earliest capital and that it was succeeded by La Venta, then Laguna de los Cerros, and finally Tres Zapotes. The large stone sculptures of the Olmec reflect this political order as well as the sequence. The large stone "altars" were actually thrones, as shown by a mural in which an Olmec ruler gestures grandly from such a sculpted seat. The famous large stone heads were apparently carved from thrones of the deceased rulers. Monuments called stelae (carved stone shafts) erected during the lifetimes of the rulers show them associated with the gods and the supernatural and as being godlike themselves. Remarkably preserved wooden busts of Olmec style and date have been found and indicate a parallel virtuosity in wood carving as well. Continual building of large platforms and presumably perishable buildings on their tops required huge efforts by the populace, as did maintenance and the ceremonies for which these buildings were the stages. Evidence of the sort of rituals that went on in these courtyards and buildings is scarce, but a group of greenstone figurines gives us a hint. These carvings were found by Heizer and his research group at La Venta (Drucker, Heizer, and Squier 1959:Figure 38) and show a row of personages lined up facing a single individual with his back to a wall formed by jadeite celts. Several people file into the space between the single person and the group. What happened next is anyone's guess, and it has been suggested that the scene is that of a coronation, a sacrifice, or an audience given by a ruler. Huge tonnages of greenstone have been found deposited at La Venta; these are interpreted simply as "work offerings," in which the labor involved was considered a good and sufficient sacrifice. The centers themselves were courtyards surrounded by clay mounds that probably had wooden structures atop them. These might have been quite magnificent; a possible analogy is the beautifully carved wooden chief's houses of the Maori. A few higher structures were probably temple platforms. Structure C-1 at La Venta is possibly one such building, and its platform is in the shape of an effigy volcano, imitating the forms of cinder cones in the nearby Tuxtla mountains.

Clearly, the elite group at the head of Olmec society had sufficient power to conscript labor for the construction projects, for the rituals, and for other labor-intensive activities. It appears that they were the first aristocrats in Mesoamerica, with their status given them by their lineage, bolstered by religious sanctions, and based on economic and political power. This archaic form of social structure, a mix of the elite caste at the top with supporting and graded classes below, was imitated, paralleled, or inherited by many other cultures in Mesoamerica, especially the Lowland Maya.

Jade jewelry became an important status symbol in itself, so much so that long-distance trade to the Balsas River area of western Mexico was developed at considerable cost. Intermediate stops in the Central Highlands of Mexico became regional centers, and at least Chalcatzingo became a residence for people from the Gulf Coast. Sculpture at the Chalcatzingo site was placed on large boulders and cliff faces. The subjects and symbolism represent a blend of the local and imported, according to the excavator of the site, David Grove (1987:434–442). A masonry throne imitating the monolithic thrones of the Gulf Coast was found as well. One stela may represent an aristocratic woman from western Mexico who married into the elite of Chalcatzingo.

Other commodities of great interest to the Olmec included obsidian from the Central Highlands and from Guatemala, probably cacao from the Pacific coast of Guatemala, and concave mirrors manufactured in Oaxaca from a locally available set of iron oxides. These long-distance contacts, combined with religious pilgrimages to the Olmec centers, stimulated the regional interaction that was so important in developing other civilized societies in Mesoamerica. These complex cultures were already taking the same evolutionary road as the Olmec, but their progress was hastened by the accelerating pace of trade and pilgrimage.

The art of the Olmec has received good press and is well known. I have already mentioned some of the political sculpture, but the art also depicted the world as generally conceived of at the time by most Mesoamericans. The large stone sculptures of the Olmec reflect this political order. The shark creature and the crocodile were incorporated into the Olmec genre and developed along specific lines. Some artistic motifs verge on writing, especially those symbols that occur on the "helmets" worn by the Olmec rulers in the great stone head sculptures. Other pictographic-type symbols also appear to carry abstract messages, but they are largely enigmatic.

The occurrence of warfare is a disputed subject, but it is pretty clear that the Olmec at least intimidated some people by force, overawed others, and negotiated with still others, largely over rights of way and access to desired commodities. Larger-than-life–sized depictions of Olmec warriors armed with clubs and often wearing feline boots occur outside the heartland and argue for something more than "friendly persuasion" in Olmec dealings with some regions.

By 400 B.C., the Olmec were no longer unique or superior in their organizational skills. These had been acquired by a number of their neighbors who either had absorbed Olmec ideas or had proceeded on parallel evolutionary tracks.

The Izapan Group of Cultures

From about 400 B.C. to A.D. 250 complex cultures were to be found not only in the former Olmec zone but also in the Maya Lowlands and Highlands, the Central Highlands of Mexico, and Oaxaca. A group of loosely related cultures who shared an art style occupied the old Olmec heartland, the Isthmus of Tehuantepec, and the Pacific coast of Guatemala. These have been labeled the Izapan cultures after the site of Izapa where there are more than 250 sculptures and carved stones, most of which are in this style.

The archaeological remains are in the form of about half a dozen large regional centers and one center so large and complex that it may have been the capital of a regional state. The regional centers are located in relatively small compartments of territory measuring several hundred square kilometers. An example of such a center is that of Abaj Takalik on the Guatemalan coast, which has a long history stretching from about 500 B.C. to perhaps A.D. 250 (Miguel Orrego, personal communication, 1992). The site began as a small regional marketing and religious center and became a political regional center dominating the zone between two rivers, the mountains, and the Pacific Ocean. Abaj Takalik consists of several courtyard groups arranged on a terraced piedmont landscape with the dramatic volcanic cones of the Guatemalan highlands on the north and the great ocean to the south. The courtyards were made up of clay platforms, which are thought to have had wooden structures on top of them; stone sculptures were placed in the central courtyards. Evidently these groups were the residences of elite families who formed the political and religious leadership of the region. They memorialized themselves by the use of stone monuments showing themselves in association with the gods and divine symbols. Strikingly, in some cases there is the use of bar-and-dot numerals and dates as in the Maya system, with one stela dating to A.D. 126. Another monument is a carved boulder with glyphs that may be much older, according to John A. Graham (1978). These dated sculptures represent the beginning of a long and rich tradition of historical records of rulers, dynasties, and states. The economic basis of the region may have been enhanced by the cash crop of cacao (chocolate) beans, which grow exceedingly well in this zone. Cacao pods are represented locally in Izapan sculpture. Later Mesoamericans regarded chocolate as a highly prestigious drink, a tradition that may go back to the Olmec.

Izapa itself is not far from Abaj Takalik, and although Izapa has more sculptures than any other Izapan site, none of them are historical-political in nature. All are pictorial and narrative and show scenes of creation and apparently many other scenes from religious sagas. These monuments were also placed in courtyards, and it may be that the resident elite families were exclusively religious in their function.

The largest site of the time and of this group of centers is that of Kaminaljuyu, which has now disappeared under present-day Guatemala City. The center again has a long history, overlapping with the latter part of the Olmec but independent and eventually going its own way. Kaminaljuyu flowered between 100 B.C. and A.D. 200, and a huge set of courtyard groups has been found scattered across a highland valley floor. As in other areas, the formal mounds were elite residences, temples, mausoleums, and the focus of various large kinship groups. Evidently, those whom we might refer to as clan leaders were housed in the groups, and the rest of the clan members lived scattered about in individual farmsteads. However, there were certainly cooperative labor arrangements, used not only to build and maintain the building groups but also to construct a huge aqueduct and a substantial irrigation system. Kaminaljuyu, with its population thought to have been in the tens of thousands, may also have controlled smaller centers such as Abaj Takalik down in the coastal plain. There are hierarchies of smaller sites around these larger ones, and it seems likely that they were subordinate to those larger in size.

Back in the old Olmec heartland, at least three regional centers took political hegemony over their districts. One was Tres Zapotes, which had a long history and may have once been a regional state capital in late Olmec history. At this center, an early historical monument (Stela C) dates to 32 B.C. in the native calendar, possibly the earliest in Mesoamerica. Cerros de las Mesas was another center that was clearly a subordinate site in Olmec times but now assumed greater power in the Izapan period. The elite at this political center gathered considerable wealth: Researchers have found 782 pieces of carved jade and greenstone pieces, four of which were Olmec heirlooms. Finally, a center called La Mojarra, unknown until recently, has produced a magnificent monument with a very long text of 520 glyphs written in a very ancient language, pre–proto-Zoque. The earliest date on the stela reads A.D. 143. The monument depicts a ruler together with hieroglyphs. The text has largely to do with his problems and intrigues in coming to power and retaining it, including difficulties created by a plot of his brother-in-law (Campbell and Kaufman 1993). The monument also shows an ancestral figure legitimizing the ruler. La Mojarra itself is not a very impressive place in terms of large buildings, but it is on the edge of a river that has eaten into the site and may have destroyed most of it, and what is left has not been excavated.

Other centers developed that show strong regional flavor in ceramics, architecture, art, and the like but that have an occasional Izapan-style monument or a few artifacts decorated in that style. The somewhat isolated site of Chiapa de Corzo is of this nature. One point of this review is that the transformed symbolism of power in Izapan times was now generally adopted by Mesoamerican elites whether or not they were directly descendant from the Olmec. Another notable development is that by A.D. 250 there were many regional variations in Mesoamerica.

The Origins of Civilization in the Valleys of Mexico and Oaxaca

Although people in the Valley of Mexico had been in touch with the Olmec by about 1300 B.C., it seems that only a few selected centers showed this influence or developed beyond a village level of life. Tlatilco and Tlapacoya were small centers that apparently furnished the Olmec with stopping points on their way to the northwest. However, these large villages had already built simple ritual structures and were using the symbols of the sacred crocodile and shark on their pottery. They also produced many other unique and beautifully made ceramics, some of them effigies of people, others of animals and fish. These items had been put into graves with persons of note, possibly lineage and clan leaders, but also with infants and children whose status must have come from their family connections alone. After about 600 B.C., there was little evidence of Olmec contact, but population growth had vastly multiplied the numbers of villages around the lakes in this highland basin. Population had gone from roughly six thousand at 900 B.C. to twenty thousand at 650 B.C. Climate and soils were superbly suitable for human agriculture, and the lakes made for easy transport. By about 400 B.C., several large villages and towns in the valley dominated the smaller communities around them and probably acted as ritual centers and markets. Cuicuilco in the southern basin had an extensive system of irrigated fields fed with lake water through a system of canals. The town probably consisted of a ritual complex of round terraced platforms with temples atop them. Several thousand people supported the town, although probably only five thousand or fewer lived in it. By 200 B.C., the population of the town and its environs had grown to about twenty thousand. These people lived in house compounds, possibly arranged on a grid pattern. The town was probably the dominant community of the Basin of Mexico by that time. However, a natural disaster intervened in what had seemed an inevitable process of further development and sophistication. About 150 B.C., a volcanic eruption covered most of the farmlands and all of the town of Cuicuilco. This is the present-day area of Mexico City known as the Pedregal.

A parallel development of population growth in the northern basin around Teotihuacan led to the division of that subvalley by 400 B.C. into six parts, each dominated by a large village or town. These are what we have more hesitantly called small and large regional centers in other zones. In this case each was fortified against its neighbors. By either violent or peaceful means, we are not sure which, the valley was unified, the defended villages on their hilltops were abandoned, and a new and very large community was established around the springs in the center of the valley: Teotihuacan.

William T. Sanders and his colleagues have studied the processes of development of civilization in the Basin of Mexico thoroughly and at length. They believe that the main element creating change was population growth (Sanders et al. 1979). This view is based largely on a narrow version of land-human relationships, with most cultural institutions regarded as epiphenomenal: frosting on the cake, so to speak. This strikes me as too restricted and too mechanistic an explanation. As will be seen in the case of the Lowland Maya, population growth indeed kicked off the move toward more complex cultures, but then a sequence of interactive factors—such as ideology, warfare, the need for water management, social structural features, and other matters—also made important contributions. It appears to be the case here as well, with cooperation and competition being the two sides to the same coin (Sanders and Price 1968). At any rate, the various elements producing civilization elsewhere in Mesoamerica were also operative here, and we leave Teotihuacan for the moment, at the threshold of becoming something quite new and much more complex than anything that had preceded it.

The Maya Lowlands

Before 1000 B.C. the tropical lowlands of the Maya area were apparently only used as a very large hunting and gathering zone. After that date, pioneer farmers began to settle along the major rivers of the south and along the Caribbean coasts of the Yucatan peninsula. These villagers were already using pottery, but it was of different kinds, indicating probable ethnic differences among the early settlers. Population growth and settlement must have been reasonably rapid, because by 600 B.C. the whole of the lowlands was filled with villages, and the people were using a sort of standardized red pottery with a waxy finish. Small clay figurines probably were used in shamanistic curing rituals. Low platforms are the only possible temple buildings at most villages, and religion seems to have been largely family and small community oriented. Most of these egalitarian villages show no signs of social differentiation.

Two exceptions, however, hint at future drastic change in these patterns. At the southern lowlands center of Nakbe, a large temple made of stone, mortar, and plaster was built about 620 B.C. (Hansen 1991), and another, which may be as old, was erected at Rio Azul. The latter temple also has large incised designs in its plaster. These two centers are about 60 km (ca. 37 miles) from one another and located on a lake and river, respectively. The structures are much too large to have been built by a village and are too sophisticated to be the first efforts at such large-scale construction. Neither shows any Olmec influence in spite of being contemporary with late Olmec sites. These temples must have been created by masses of people from a number of villages who were somehow persuaded and organized for the effort. The implication is that there was some type of elite leadership in being, although they may have been still of the category that we know as "complex chiefdoms" (Wright 1994). These were historically to be found in Polynesia and were capable of large-scale building efforts of the same kind as at Nakbe and Rio Azul. In other words, state-level organization had not yet been developed. We can confidently call these places *large regional centers* of the kind that appeared in the Central Valley of Oaxaca at about the same time and in the Valley of Mexico later.

In the case of the Maya, the potential for social control existed because of the need for stored water for the annual drought of at least 120 days from February to May. This is a climatic characteristic of the tropical forests of Central America. If larger-than-village-sized human populations were to survive year-round in these zones, then large reservoirs were needed to carry them through the long dry seasons. Leadership groups seized upon these possibilities and organized large numbers of people to create water storage facilities and then apparently also used control over the people to bolster and cement their own superior status. Whether the need for larger water storage facilities drove the development of more complex social organization or the need for more concentrated populations in order to build religious structures motivated the growth of large centers is still undetermined. What is certain is that although population fluctuation constantly occurred, it was only one of a series of factors that interacted to produce the particular features of Lowland Maya civilization.

By 250 B.C., the landscape was filled with large numbers of villages, small and large centers, and some megacenters, five of which are known. With one exception, all were located on large shallow lakes; from north to south they were Edzna, Calakmul, El Mirador, Tikal, and Tayasal. Edzna was exceptional—its water supply was guaranteed by an immense canal in the center of a large shallow valley and by feeder ditches dug along the sides of the valley. Each of these five sites is distinguished by access to water and also by huge buildings erected during the 500-year period from 250 B.C. to A.D. 250. Calakmul and Tikal both have very large temples dating from the period; measured by bulk, El Mirador has probably the largest structures ever built in the Maya area. Clearly, by 250 B.C., the Maya had developed an elite class capable of mustering huge amounts of manpower for construction. Further, by the end of the period, most important centers were also fortified, indicating competition among the leadership groups and the rise of organized violence.

Tikal is one of the best known in terms of early fortifications, and its dry moat and parapet systems total about 25 km (15.5 miles) in length (see Figure 2.2). The center is located on a ridge between two large swamps that lie to the east and west. These are natural barriers filled with thorny vines and trees, marshy ground, and canal networks, all of which would also exact a high price in time and disorganization from any military force trying to move through them. The northern and southern approaches are covered by defensive lines. These fortifications are so long that the best means of utilizing them would be by a defense in depth with patrols, outposts, main line defensive points, and "fire brigades." All of this bespeaks the possibility of a remarkable sophistication in tactics.

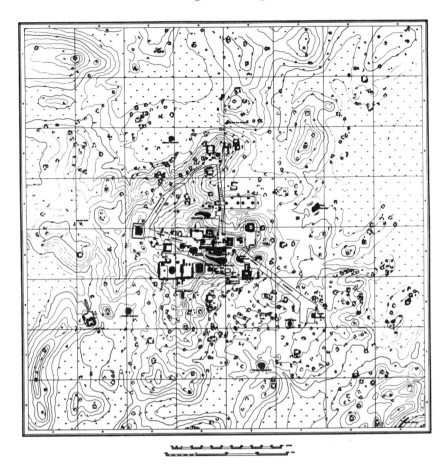

FIGURE 2.2   Schematic map of the city of Tikal, Guatemala. (Courtesy of the University of Pennsylvania Museum of Archaeology and Ethnology.)

The Late Preclassic fortress of Becan is more compact and the defenses more formidable in that the moats are deeper and the parapets steeper. Inside are very steep and defensible buildings with towers. This center is more like the medieval castles of Europe with their outlying walls and inner keeps. El Mirador depended on its massive basal platforms and walls, whereas Calakmul was surrounded by difficult swampy terrain and had massive walls. Edzna, in the north, had a fortified keep or citadel located in the major canal and surrounded by water. All of these military features bespeak a period of intense competition between elites who had gained control of their respective regions. The myth of the "peaceful Maya" is far from the realities that are reflected early in the record. Eventually, several centers either dropped out of competition or became quiescent. Tayasal seems to have lost its political base. Not all failures were political or military, however. El Mirador was probably abandoned because its shallow lakes went dry. This ecological disaster foreshadowed the continued and finally catastrophic problems that would overwhelm later Maya civilization.

By A.D. 250, the Maya had achieved fully civilized status, with several large capital cities, several levels of subordinate administrative centers, a controlling elite who formed an aristocracy, intensive food production partly based on wetland gardening, and a capable and vigorous military system. State-level political systems organized the lowlands into a number of competitive local and regional units. Tens of thousands of commoners supported aristocrats who traced their descent from the gods and recorded their genealogies and portraits on stone sculpture. Writing, calendars, and complex art glorified the upper classes. Immense efforts created grandiose temples to the ancestors and gods and provided burial places for rulers and their relatives. Multiroomed structures functioned as palatial residences for the elites as well as offices and other administrative rooms. Acres of pavement were created by the use of high quality plaster over graded ballasts of stone, gravel, and pebbles.

The remaining forests went down under the increasing impact of farming, construction, and woodcutting. The slaked lime needed for mortar and plaster required huge amounts of fuel to burn off the impurities from raw limestone. Fifty small trees were required for each commoner family house, and thus a thousand families generated a demand for fifty thousand trees. More people were required for the state enterprises of monumental architecture, warfare, and intensive food production. Demitri Shimkin (personal communication, 1970) has pointed out that state-level societies for these and other reasons tend to encourage population growth. The controlling elites have their own agendas. They want people to do construction labor, fill up the armies, act as servants, and carry out countless tasks that aristocrats seem to have no difficulty in imagining. It seems to have been so in the Maya case and is an example of the interactive nature of the various evolutionary factors involved in the creation of a civilization.

We leave the Maya at the end of their first florescence and return to the Valley of Mexico, where developments occurred in the early part of the Christian era that would affect all of Mesoamerica.

Teotihuacan

One of the most remarkable civilizations in Mesoamerica was located in a subvalley opening to the northeast from the Basin of Mexico. Although the southern basin has always been the most agriculturally desirable zone, it was badly damaged about 150 B.C. by a volcanic eruption. The precocious city of Cuicuilco lost its fields, canal systems, and finally houses and buildings. After the fiery demise of its competitor city, Teotihuacan was able to dictate its own development. Its subsequent history appears to be in great part the fulfillment of rationalized plans and much less a situation of growth modified by circumstance as seen so often in history. One early and deliberate policy was that of population resettlement from the rest of the basin into one great urban complex at Teotihuacan (R. Millon 1988:103). This movement resulted in an increase from about 2,000 people in 200 B.C. to about 60,000 at A.D. 100. Later, by A.D. 550, the city would have 125,000 inhabitants, making it one of the six largest cities in the world at the time.

The City

The urban structure of this civilization is also remarkable and reflects the nature and patterns of Teotihuacan culture (see Figure 2.3). The city covers about 20.7 km² (8 mi²) and is oriented along two axes, one running roughly north-south (the Street of the Dead) and the other east-west. Near the north end of the Street of the Dead are the two largest buildings in the city, the Temples of the Sun and the Moon. The Pyramid of the Sun is also the largest temple in the city. It was sited over a sacred cave that might be one of those associated with the creation myths. Rene Millon (1981:230) suggests that Teotihuacan was "the place where time began" as mentioned by Sahagun's sixteenth-century informants (1950–1970). (The reader is cautioned that most of the names of structures, barrios, and streets at Teotihuacan were given either by the later Aztecs, archaeologists, or tourist guides.) Many other temples, crowded along the principal avenue, indicate that the city was a great religious center. It was also a cosmopolitan city with a large marketplace, an administrative compound for the ruler (the Citadel), palaces, and commoner housing standardized in certain features, but not in plan or size.

At the beginning of the city's history, the most common housing was a somewhat chaotic scatter of adobe structures around the major com-

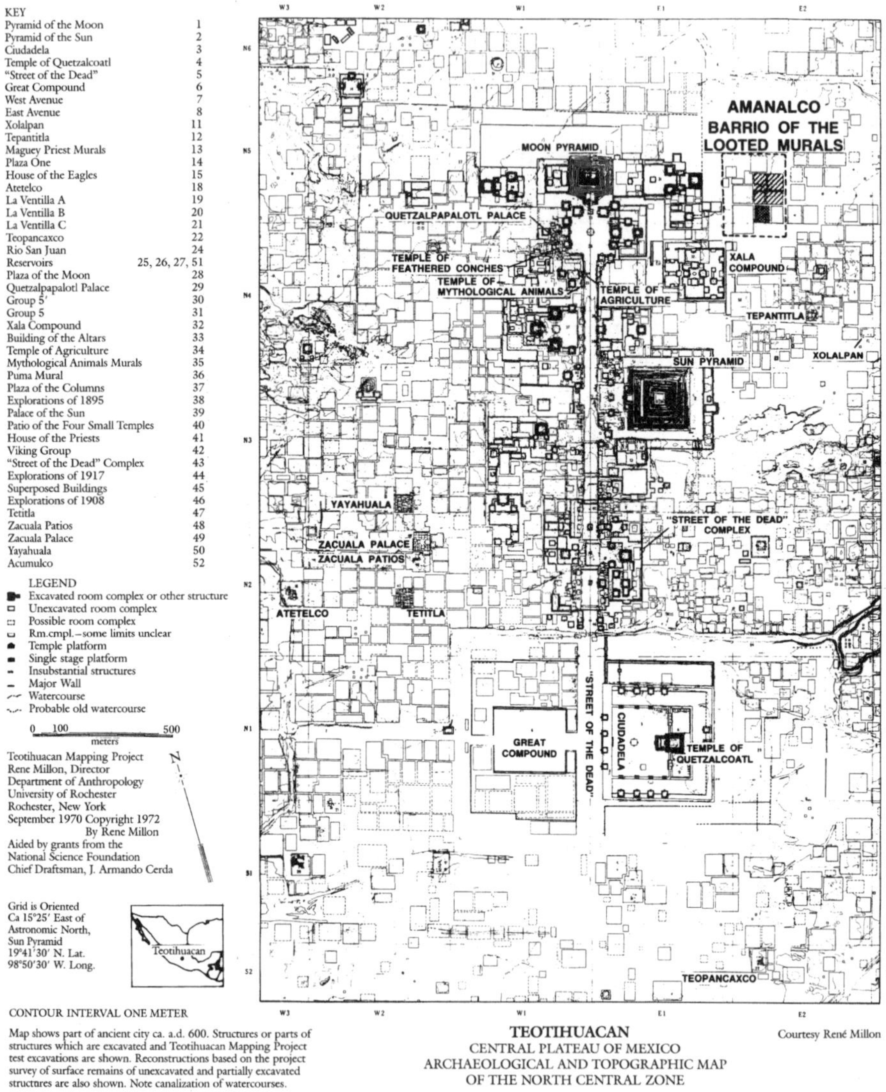
KEY
Pyramid of the Moon 1
Pyramid of the Sun 2
Ciudadela 3
Temple of Quetzalcoatl 4
"Street of the Dead" 5
Great Compound 6
West Avenue 7
East Avenue 8
Xolalpan 11
Tepantitla 12
Maguey Priest Murals 13
Plaza One 14
House of the Eagles 15
Atetelco 18
La Ventilla A 19
La Ventilla B 20
La Ventilla C 21
Teopancaxco 22
Rio San Juan 24
Reservoirs 25, 26, 27, 51
Plaza of the Moon 28
Quetzalpapalotl Palace 29
Group 5' 30
Group 5 31
Xala Compound 32
Building of the Altars 33
Temple of Agriculture 34
Mythological Animals Murals 35
Puma Mural 36
Plaza of the Columns 37
Explorations of 1895 38
Palace of the Sun 39
Patio of the Four Small Temples 40
House of the Priests 41
Viking Group 42
"Street of the Dead" Complex 43
Explorations of 1917 44
Superposed Buildings 45
Explorations of 1908 46
Tetitla 47
Zacuala Patios 48
Zacuala Palace 49
Yayahuala 50
Acumulco 52
LEGEND
Excavated room complex or other structure
Unexcavated room complex
Possible room complex
Rm.cmpl.–some limits unclear
Temple platform
Single stage platform
Insubstantial structures
Major Wall
Watercourse
Probable old watercourse
0 100 500
meters
Teotihuacan Mapping Project
Rene Millon, Director
Department of Anthropology
University of Rochester
Rochester, New York
September 1970 Copyright 1972
By Rene Millon
Aided by grants from the
National Science Foundation
Chief Draftsman, J. Armando Cerda
N
Grid is Oriented
Ca 15°25' East of
Astronomic North,
Sun Pyramid
19°41'30' N. Lat.
98°50'30' W. Long.
Teotihuacan
CONTOUR INTERVAL ONE METER
Map shows part of ancient city ca. a.d. 600. Structures or parts of structures which are excavated and Teotihuacan Mapping Project test excavations are shown. Reconstructions based on the project survey of surface remains of unexcavated and partially excavated structures are also shown. Note canalization of watercourses.
W3
W2
W1
E1
E2
N6
N5
N4
N3
N2
N1
S1
S2
AMANALCO
BARRIO OF THE
LOOTED MURALS
MOON PYRAMID
QUETZALPAPALOTL PALACE
TEMPLE OF
FEATHERED CONCHES
TEMPLE OF
MYTHOLOGICAL ANIMALS
TEMPLE OF
AGRICULTURE
XALA
COMPOUND
TEPANTITLA
XOLALPAN
SUN PYRAMID
YAYAHUALA
ZACUALA PALACE
ZACUALA PATIOS
"STREET OF THE DEAD"
COMPLEX
ATETELCO
TETITLA
GREAT
COMPOUND
"STREET OF THE DEAD"
CIUDADELA
TEMPLE OF
QUETZALCOATL
TEOPANCAXCO
TEOTIHUACAN
CENTRAL PLATEAU OF MEXICO
ARCHAEOLOGICAL AND TOPOGRAPHIC MAP
OF THE NORTH CENTRAL ZONE
Courtesy René Millon

FIGURE 2.3 City plan of Teotihuacan, Mexico. (Courtesy of René Millon.)

pounds and avenues. In the fourth century A.D., however, commoner housing was reorganized by being laid out on a rough grid oriented on the avenues, and what had been individual residential units were aggregated into apartment compounds. These compounds vary greatly in plan and size, but all have similar components. The main structure consists of a high wall surrounding the interior room complexes. These major walls, 2.4 to 3 m (8 to 10 feet) high, enclosed clusters of rooms that formed apartments, each having a kitchen and sleeping quarters. Two or more of the apartments opened onto interior courtyards, and the larger room clusters incorporated light wells. All the construction was of high quality mortar; large chunks of volcanic rock were set into the mortar, and then the whole structure was plastered. Each of the compounds had a system of underfloor drains built before the walls and plaster floors were laid (R. Millon 1988:108). All buildings were flat roofed by the beam-and-mortar method, that is, with large timbers laid from wall to wall as supports for a roof of wooden framework and mortar skin. As in the case of the Maya, construction must have demanded huge amounts of wood and have led to deforestation in the immediate vicinity.

Although over two thousand apartment compounds are known, only about fifteen have been excavated to date. All of these have produced polychrome wall murals that range from mediocre to magnificent in quality but are all of great interest. Over the three hundred years during which the compounds were built, rebuilt, and redecorated, artistic norms shifted and changed. For the most part, however, subject matter remained the same through time (C. Millon 1973). Many of the murals are pictures of the gods, god impersonators, or religious ceremonies. Priests or gods hold out their hands, from which flow all sorts of desirable items. In other such scenes, worshippers sit or stand around an altar with smoking incense burners. In some of the most interesting, priests cross planted fields shaking aspergilla and blessing the crops, which in one case are century plants. Other paintings appear to reflect actual life scenes, but they may be from the afterlife—in a word, paradise. People play games, sing, and chase butterflies amid irrigated fields. Butterflies are thought to represent souls of the dead. There are a fair number of abstract murals whose ultimate meaning is presently unattainable to us: netted jaguars, interlaced with morning glories and associated with starfish, for example. There are also about fifty elements that may be glyphs, especially those from the Barrio of the Looted Murals. In these paintings, several military officers are shown with glyphs that are almost certainly their names. Clara Millon

(1973) has pointed out that the tassel was the symbol and perhaps even the phonetic name for Teotihuacan. Depictions of military subjects increase toward the end of Teotihuacan's history; for example, warriors are shown dancing with human hearts on the ends of their knives or simply striding along in battle dress.

What we see now is the skeleton of the city, peopled only by visitors, looters, and guards. Once, however, it was bright with painted colors on the buildings, which also sported wooden frameworks with waving feathers and pieces of cloth. Murals also decorated the exteriors of structures, especially the recessed panels (*tableros*) so characteristic of Teotihuacan architecture. Throngs of people, native and visitors alike, must have passed daily into the dozens of temples, burning incense and making other offerings. Many apartment compounds also had their own altars for home worship. Craft specialists plied their trades, working obsidian and producing pottery, and there were huge numbers of construction workers. These artisans lived and worked in the apartment compounds, as did the farmers who produced the immense amounts of food needed. The palaces that provided housing and offices for the elite and their dependents are located along the principal north-south avenue. A number of these complex buildings are associated with the major temples, many of which are surrounded by embankments. The largest palace complex of all is located in the Citadel complex, itself within an embankment originally surmounted by walls. The most elaborate temple of the city is also located here, and the earliest version of it is decorated with serpent and feline heads, with much marine symbolism provided by seashell decorations. Recent excavations of the temple have uncovered more than two hundred sacrificial victims, apparently war captives, found in association with several large and rich burials. Perhaps the latter represent the original rulers of Teotihuacan, memorialized by the temple and accompanied by the human sacrificial offerings. The Great Compound, now the location of the tourist center and bus parking area, is directly across the north-south avenue from the Citadel. Rene Millon's work (1981) indicates that this was the principal market of the city.

Militarism and Trade

The role of militarism was strong from the beginning of Teotihuacan's rise but was masked in early centuries by the emphasis on religious symbolism and function (R. Millon 1988:109). Murals depicting warriors have been noted, but major evidence for Teotihuacan militarism is also found in far-flung areas in Mesoamerica, particularly in the Maya areas to the east. The main reason for the use of force appears to have been to secure trade routes and access to commodities. Cacao beans from the Pacific coast of Guatemala, tropical bird feathers from the highlands and lowlands, salt from the lagoons of northern Yucatan, honey from the peninsula, and medicinal herbs from the Lowland Maya tropical forests were among the most important commodities. We examine specific instances of political and military domination in the next section, but Teotihuacan dealt with the Maya politically, militarily, and diplomatically.

In the city itself, evidence of resident foreigners has been found, especially in the Merchants Barrio and the Oaxacan Barrio. In both cases, excavated evidence shows the presence of persons of foreign culture who brought with them their own customs and artifacts. Lowland Maya polychrome pottery has been found in the Merchants Barrio associated with keyhole-shaped houses that may have functioned as both residences and warehouses (Rattray 1987). A Zapotec, perhaps a merchant, died, and a Zapotec tomb was built for him in the Oaxaca Barrio, complete with Zapotec-style sculpture and funerary urn (R. Millon 1988:108). In both the Maya and Zapotec cases we have reciprocal evidence of Teotihuacan contact from the respective homelands. At least two other foreign ethnic groups resided in Teotihuacan: Huaxtec from the northeast and Totonac from the Gulf Coast to the southeast of the basin.

In fact, although this pattern is clearest in the cases of foreign residents, apartment compounds grouped into barrios appear to have been basic administrative units in the city. Rene Millon notes that "a barrio where people of relatively high rank . . . may have lived" is located in the northeast part of the city and may have been the residential zone for high-ranking military officers (1988:108).

The subsistence base for the city was the entire Basin of Mexico and adjacent zones such as Tlaxcala, to the east. Huge amounts of food were required and could have been produced from the best lands in the southern part of the basin, partly by using the drained/raised-field system of wetland gardening. This system involved the canal drainage of swamps and often entailed the creation of artificial platforms for growing plants between canals. More conventional irrigation agriculture was undoubtedly practiced as well as slash-and-burn cultivation on steeper slopes. Tribute from other zones must have supplemented foodstuffs produced regionally. Rene Millon suggests that the core area for Teotihuacan was about 25,900 km² (10,000 mi²) with a total population of between 300,000 and 500,000 (1988:113). Specialty farming villages also produced crops such as maguey (the century plant cactus), which was the source of fiber for rough cloth and rope as well as of *pulque*, a fermented and mildly alcoholic drink.

Teotihuacan's Links with Other Cultures

In the Maya area there are two clear cases of Teotihuacan contact. One is at the south highland center of Kaminaljuyu, already noted as a giant center during the Late Preclassic. At some point in the fourth century A.D., Teotihuacan took over the center and physically reorganized it into a more nucleated group of temples, elite residences, and administrative offices. Although there is no population fluctuation at this time, the impression is strong of a radical change in leadership as well as in political structure. Temples built during this period were adobe imitations of the style of building current at Teotihuacan itself. Population appears to have been concentrated, probably for greater social and political control, as in the home territories. Geography would permit Kaminaljuyu to control the nearby Pacific coast and its cacao-growing zones. Such control was probably the motivation for the complete takeover by the Teotihuacan military, in contrast to other Mesoamerican zones where diplomatic relations seem to have been enough (R. Millon 1988:122–123).

In the Maya Lowlands, at the already great city of Tikal, we are fortunate to have a series of well-documented burials and other archaeological data that correlates with texts written in Maya script. According to this evidence, contact was made by A.D. 360 and was probably through long-distance traders from Teotihuacan who arrived at Tikal. In later times, such traders were often intelligence agents for the state, and such may have been the case here. Tikal was one of the largest of the Maya cities at the time, with a population of about twenty-five thousand, and the capital of a regional state with subordinate cities. It was possibly this degree of organization that attracted the Teotihuacanos, but in any case, they came, they saw, and they eventually conquered. Clemency Coggins (1979) reads the evidence as follows: In Tikal in A.D. 378, a ruler nicknamed Jaguar Paw II by archaeologists was displaced by a Maya noble nicknamed Curl-Nose, who was a close ally of Teotihuacan. It is tempting to believe that a palace coup may have been engineered behind the scenes by Teotihuacan, with a stooge ruler being placed on the throne at this powerful Maya city.

Tikal began an expansion that led it in about one hundred years to the status of the largest Maya regional state. Curl-Nose's son is shown on Tikal stela 31 flanked by two armed Teotihuacan warriors. Military assistance and political advice from resident Teotihuacan councilors were crucial in Tikal's further expansion. Its enemy to the northwest, Calakmul, was blocked for the time being, and the northeast frontier was stabilized along the Rio Azul. The Tikal regional state may have covered as much as 50,000 km^2 (19,300 mi^2) at this time, one-fifth of the entire lowlands. The dynasty established by Curl-Nose evidently continued until A.D. 534, when a series of drastic changes occurred—among them, the withdrawal of Teotihuacan from the Maya Lowlands. Two other Maya cities and a possible battlefield also have Teotihuacan-related monuments.

In Oaxaca, the Zapotec state had been established by 200 B.C. with a capital at Monte Alban. Five hundred years later, after a long series of conquests that expanded the polity outside the Central Valley of Oaxaca, Teotihuacan contacted the Zapotecs. By A.D. 300, there was a Oaxacan barrio in Teotihuacan, although Rene Millon notes that the residents do not seem to have been of high status (1988:129). At Monte Alban, however, contacts were on the highest levels. Unarmed persons from Teotihuacan are shown on five sculptures engaging in "diplomatic encounters" with the Zapotec elite (Marcus 1983). This was clearly a different type of relationship than that with the Maya groups. Possibly, Monte Alban, with its tradition of aggressive militarism and secure within its mountain fastness, was not worth the risks and costs to conquer.

In other parts of Mesoamerica, particularly the northwest and west, Teotihuacan seems to have been interested only in the local resources and did just what was needed to secure them. In Zacatecas, for example, there are extensive even if shallow mines and miners' camps from the period. In terms of cultural evolution, Teotihuacan played the same role as the earlier Olmecs although on a larger scale and with more options. Both cultures acted to accelerate cultural change and development as well as to intensify the contacts among the various cultures of the area.

Monte Alban and the Classic Zapotecs of Oaxaca

In Oaxaca, a long-term regional project has produced a convincing evolutionary sequence of cultures for the central valley (Flannery and Marcus 1983). By about 1400 B.C. a series of widely spaced, independent villages with their dependent hamlets was scattered along the valley's major rivers.

These probably were using a sort of family-style irrigation system known as "pot irrigation" that is still practiced today in the zone. In this case, the fields are long and rectangular and edged with regularly spaced wells that reach to the shallow water table. Each plant is watered with a pot of water drawn from the nearest well, a task well within the capacities of nearly every member of a family. It will be recalled that this zone was in at least indirect contact with the Olmec and made the famous concave mirrors exported to the Gulf Coast centers. No other Olmec linkage is plausible.

Gradual population growth transformed some communities into regional centers, one of which was San Jose Mogote. This center had about thirteen hundred inhabitants by 500 B.C. and served as a market, ritual, and administrative place for its zone. By 100 B.C., seven petty states had emerged, each with its capital, each with its resident elite, and all with their hierarchy of subordinate communities. These states appear to have been competitive, and it is in this context that the first writing and sculpture appear. In a building at San Jose Mogote a large slab of stone was put down as a doorsill; on it was carved the image of a named captive who had been sacrificed. This is the earliest of a class of war memorials that would be very common at one of the seven large regional centers, the emergent capital of Monte Alban.

A New Capital

Monte Alban won the competition among the seven Preclassic petty states and established its control over the entire Valley of Oaxaca. This center was in a strategic location, and it was here that much of the valley's population was concentrated into what would become the largest city in Oaxaca and the capital of a conquest state. Over three hundred so-called *danzante* (dancing figure) sculptures are to be found on top of the heavily modified ridge at the center of the valley; each is a celebration of a victory over an enemy. Each loser is named, shown humiliated (that is, without finery), and most of the time also shown mutilated and dead. By 100 B.C. fortification walls were built. These data suggest that Monte Alban won its place by military means. However, Richard Blanton (1978) believes that "friendly persuasion" was used to create a confederacy of the various petty states, who voluntarily gave up their independence for the greater good. Although this appears to be against human nature and the historical record, there is something to be said for the theory.

Once established as the dominant center after 200 B.C., Monte Alban developed into a city on the terraced slopes of its three ridges. The city appears to have been divided into various sectors (barrios), and each may have been represented in the central precincts of the city by a major temple. This evidence is somewhat ambiguous, however, and the arrangement may be interpreted as evidence of either a negotiated resettlement or a conciliatory gesture after the trauma of forcible coalition. In any case, Monte Alban grew from about 5,000 people at 200 B.C. to 24,000 by A.D. 550.

By A.D. 250 the Zapotecs had conquered areas outside the Central Valley of Oaxaca and set up a different style of conquest monuments to commemorate victories. Some of these forty subjugated places can be identified because they still use the same names today that they did in the prehistoric past. These names link them with later Aztec and earlier Zapotec hieroglyphs. Marcus suggests that these forty names define a kind of perimeter of control (Marcus 1980). However, militarism seems to have carried the Zapotecs only to distances of perhaps 50 km (31 miles) away from their home valley, and thereafter their actions became defensive.

The nature of the elite class that had emerged by A.D. 250 was clearly political and religiously sanctioned. Military leadership was also clearly an important role for the upper classes. Stone tombs within the center appear as early as 200 B.C. or before. After A.D. 250, tombs are much more elaborate, placed in major structures, and sometimes decorated with murals. These final resting places of the elite also were chock-full of pottery, much of which probably contained food at the time of the funeral. The famous Zapotec funerary urns made of pottery appear and may be portraits of apotheosized ancestors, some of whom wear gods' masks. Other elaborate ceramics also were put into the tombs as final offerings. Retainers and/or servants were also buried with their masters. By this time the Zapotec elite probably had assumed a semidivine status similar to that which they held at the time of the Spanish conquest and required the kind of entourage in the afterlife that they had enjoyed in this world.

The Great Period of Zapotec Culture

By A.D. 550, Monte Alban sprawled for 39 km² (15 mi²) over three connected and terraced ridges and contained about twenty-four thousand people housed in apartment compounds, similar to but smaller than those at Teotihuacan. Each compound rested on a terrace that provided both a flattened construction site as well as space for a kitchen garden. Apparently most or all had their own cistern or small reservoir created by block-ing a nearby gully. These residences were grouped, as noted before, into wards (fourteen during this period), each with its own temple and civic structures and some connected one to another by roads. Interestingly, none of the roads lead to the most important precinct above, the ridge where the rulers lived. There were also fifty-seven elaborate buildings that were aristocratic residences. These are better constructed than the ordi-nary apartment compounds, with more rooms and more space in the rooms. Based on the frequency of the housing of the nobility, Flannery (1983:136) estimates that they represented about 4 percent of the popula-tion.

One hundred seventy tombs were found at the site, most of which date to this period. Some are located in the Main Plaza atop the ridge, but most are located under the patio floors of the apartment compounds and of the palaces. Some of these tombs had become family mausoleums by this time; new bodies and offerings were often placed in them. The murals occasionally found on tomb walls are lively and some show rituals in which gaily costumed lines of figures walk along chanting, singing, or talking. Marcus (1983a) has pointed out that there is an emphasis on royal couples in the art of all kinds now, contrasted to the earlier emphasis on military males. The incense burners found in the tombs had become very elaborate by this time, and Caso and Bernal (1952) defined thirty-nine different gods by studying their iconography. Some of these gods un-doubtedly are deities, but some are likely the transfigured family ancestral spirits, as Marcus (1983a) has suggested.

Atop the ridge, and atop society both physically and socially, lived the rulers of Monte Alban. The top of the ridge had been further modified and expanded by this time to accommodate fifteen building complexes, includ-ing a ball court. The alignment of the Main Plaza is roughly north-south, with a huge platform at each end. The southern platform supports what appears to be the largest temple at the site, never excavated. The impor-tance of the structure is obvious both from its size and from the fact that most of the sculptures showing Teotihuacan visits were placed at its cor-ners although not publicly displayed. Including the hidden monuments, there were at least eighteen stelae, most in the Main Plaza but some on the North Platform. The North Platform is composed of the largest palace in the city and undoubtedly was the residence of the rulers and their families. Again, the superstructures are elevated on a massive basal platform; access was through a portico structure at the top of a grand staircase.

The function of this building was control of access to the rest of the complex, and it is a fairly widespread type of structure in Mesoamerica. Porters and guards would have been posted here. Above and inside, there is a poorly understood series of inner courtyards, temples, and residential buildings that probably included administrative rooms. Although the style is distinct, the functional elements of the complex would have been understandable to a later Aztec or a contemporary Lowland Maya. From here, then, a succession of divine kings and aristocrats ruled for generations over the Central Valley and far beyond it. A few medium-sized and many small administrative centers handled the day-to-day tasks of keeping the state functioning and the rulers informed. For centuries, this was a successful political and economic system, but the time came when it broke apart.

Classic Maya Civilization

The Lowland Maya had achieved civilized status by 250 B.C. and possibly before. They had developed sophisticated organization for dealing with the problems of yearly drought, feeding tens of thousands of people, political organization, and security of the state. Leadership was vested in an aristocratic elite whose high status was religiously sanctioned. Intermarriage among the ruling families of the regional states and city-states made for integration and cross linkage, although not necessarily for peace. Large building projects kept the masses busy during the lengthy periods of time not required for agriculture and resulted in the awe-inspiring temples and palaces. The former were the burial places of rulers and their families, and the palaces were where they lived and administered. Large numbers of servants and retainers were required for daily tasks of cleaning, cooking, and so forth, but retinues of retainers also served the rulers and the state. These people were the higher and petty administrators, the varied kinds of priests, and soldiery and their officers as well as a great many specialized craftsmen and artisans.

Long-distance trade kept the Maya rulers supplied with such luxury and status items as jade, feathers of the iridescent quetzal bird, and cacao; trade also kept them in touch with the distant civilizations of the Maya and Mexican highlands. We have seen how Teotihuacan traders contacted the Maya at the capital city of Tikal and how that led to an alliance with political, economic, and military benefits for both sides. The Tikal regional state became large, powerful, and expansive. However, the Tikal rulers had developed both internal and external enemies. Tikal's expansion had apparently been partly at the expense of the large regional state of Calakmul to its northwest. Ever after, for the next five hundred years, whoever was Tikal's enemy was potentially a friend of Calakmul (Marcus and Folan 1994).

The Maya Hiatus (A.D. 534–660)

One of the most enigmatic events in the history of Mesoamerica is the sudden break in historical records of the Maya, a break that begins abruptly at A.D. 534 and lasts at most sites for at least sixty years (to A.D. 593) and in some places such as Tikal and Rio Azul for 120 years. The nature of the event is as yet uncertain, but based on recent climatic research, a very long, dry, cool period occurred that had disastrous effects on food production (Gill 1994). One possibility is that of a gigantic volcanic eruption with immense sulfur content that drastically altered the intensity of sunlight for a year or two. El Chichón volcano in southeastern Mexico is a candidate, with its history of recent and ancient eruptions and the highly sulfuric content of its ash and other ejecta. Another recently discovered possibility is the comet impact that created the Chubb crater in northern Quebec, Canada (Keys 1994). This impact took place in A.D. 534 or 535, according to associated tree-ring dates, and the comet was three times larger than the largest fragment of Shoemaker-Levy 9 that hit Jupiter in August 1994. The effects of the sixth-century impact were worldwide and noted by Old World historians such as Procopius, John of Lydia, and Cassiodorus. Chinese scholars recorded massive droughts and famines from A.D. 536 to 538, and in A.D. 534 the emperor ordered the evacuation of the 1.5 million people living in the capital and its environs. The question remains as to whether the comet impact had a secondary volcanic effect or if it itself threw enough sulfur into the atmosphere to achieve catastrophic results.

Whatever caused the interruption of Maya dynastic records, the mass of the population also was affected. Depopulation of the countryside occurred in widespread zones, according to recent research. For this or other reasons, Teotihuacan withdrew from its most distant outposts in Mesoamerica. For those Lowland Maya allied with the great empire, the withdrawal led to political difficulties. The descendants of the displaced rulers of Tikal apparently chose this moment to attempt a comeback, with resultant civil wars (Coggins 1979). The result was not only an exacerbation of the effect of the disaster on food production but also political and military chaos. For example, Tikal's frontier fortress city, Rio Azul, was overrun and burned at this time, and although it was eventually resuscitated, it never regained the importance that it once had.

The Maya Late Classic

The hiatus had some profound effects. The large regional states, which had evidently been built on the model of Teotihuacan during the Early Classic, gave way to a more fragmented political picture. City-states and smaller regional states dominated the Late Classic, with many usurpers, pretenders, and others apparently trying to carve out territories for themselves. At Rio Azul, the first historical monument erected after the hiatus dates to A.D. 661 and names a governor who claims the title of an independent ruler (Bacab). Tikal recovered, buffered by its great resources, and the first great ruler, a man named Ah Cacau (Jones and Satterthwaite 1982), claimed descent from the usurper Curl-Nose. Thus, the older ruling families failed in their attempt at recapturing power, and the descendants of the Teotihuacan-linked rulers triumphed.

Ah Cacau or Ruler A came to power in A.D. 681 and began a program of building gigantic temples and palace structures that was carried on by his successors until it reached megalomaniac proportions. These constructions absorbed ever more energy and resources. At the same time, from A.D. 650 onward, the Rio Azul–La Milpa region shows a surge in population growth on the order of 2 to 3 percent per year (Adams et al. 1997). This is an exponential rate of growth, which means a doubling of numbers every twenty-four to thirty-seven years. Possibly this was state-sponsored growth for reasons of manpower needed for projects such as construction, warfare, food production, and other items on the elite agenda. Possibly it was also largely an immigrant population from other regions. Tikal reached a population of 80,000 by A.D. 750 (Culbert et al. 1990), a very large figure for a preindustrial city. To put things in perspective, the population of sixteenth-century London was 50,000, and large towns in England at that time were 3,500 to 5,000 in size (Platt 1979:19). Tikal's great rival, Calakmul, grew as well, to a size of about 50,000 people in a city surrounded by swamp gardens.

Although neither regional state regained the sizes of the Early Classic states, both attempted to compensate through a series of alliances that are recorded in dynastic records. These records are complex, suspect as propaganda, and even inaccurate (Marcus 1992). However, they give the general tone of political and military affairs of the time. Warfare seems to have been a matter of sputtering and sporadic conflict between these states, often conducted through surrogates (Marcus and Folan 1994:24).

In spite of regional and local conflicts, this last period was one of great and splendid growth of Maya civilization. Copan, a capital of a small regional state on the southeastern edge of the lowlands, produced huge amounts of sculpture that decorated not only its historical monuments but especially its buildings. It is almost as if the rulers, although provincial, had to demonstrate their membership in the Maya Classic by excessive use of its symbols. The whole Valley of Copan sustained only 25,000 people at its maximum population levels, but clearly the rulers made the most of their chances and created a beautiful and impressive capital center.

The same phenomenal growth took place at Palenque, in the Rio Bec region, and in other parts of the Maya Lowlands. One suspects that exceptionally favorable climatic conditions and the achievement of what Vernon Scarborough (1994) calls an "accretionary landscape" were important factors. Scarborough has shown that the Late Classic Maya lived in an almost totally engineered landscape, modified over centuries and dozens of generations by unremitting toil and planning. The first steps had been taken by 500 B.C.; slowly, nearly all landscape features had been affected by human activity. The Maya channelized watercourses, terraced hillsides, flattened ridge tops, and created water management systems to make maximum use of the resource that was cut off each year for three or four months. Although extraordinarily effective, this system of land use was also very vulnerable to climatic change and other perturbations.

The aristocrats of the lowlands in many zones took advantage of the decentralization of political authority to grab land and power for themselves in a way similar to that occurring in Europe as the Roman empire came to an end. The result was also similar in that a feudal order of society was created. Small and large country estates developed with client peasant families living in clusters around the manor houses or minor palaces. The Rio Bec, Rio Azul, and La Milpa zones show this process as does Copan, which appears to have lost its king to war, his successor then apparently having ceded power to his principal nobles. Population was spread thickly over the countryside as well as in proximity to urban centers. At the same time, refuge fortresses were built in insecure regions such as around Rio Azul. The nearby Late Classic fortress of Kinal was built on a ridge and never taken (Adams 1991).

Writing, Mathematics, Calendrics

Meanwhile, in the cities, the Maya continued to develop the abstract bodies of knowledge and intellectual skills that have made them famous among world cultures. Their system of mathematics was based on units of 20 rather than units of 10 (our decimal system). They used positional notation, but usually in vertical arrangement. A notation system of dots for units of one and bars for units of five was backed up by the concept of zero. Calendrical cycles based on days nested within one another, each larger one incorporating the smaller units. For example, a *kin* was a single day; a *uinal* was a unit of twenty days. At this point the Maya introduced an irregularity for the sake of pulling the calendrical system into better alignment with the solar year and multiplied the *uinal* by 18 rather than 20 to produce the next unit, a *tun* of 360 days. Ever larger cycles provided the possibility of calculating through infinity, one that the Maya enthusiastically exploited. Such calculations are recorded in certain texts, largely for the purpose of dealing with cycles of creation. Historical events were recorded in terms of time elapsed since a base date equivalent to our 3114 B.C. This may have represented the beginning of a new cycle of creation, but in any case leads to dates that are accurate to the day. Thus a "normal" date of 9.17.0.0.0 means that 9 units of 144,000 days and 17 units of 7,200 days have passed since the "start of time." This is equivalent to the Christian chronology of 30 November A.D. 780. In addition, the Maya also added on the date in the "sacred almanac," a cycle of 260 days and 18 months. Because of mathematical permutations, this calendar repeated itself each 52 years and thus was a weak reed to lean on for recording long-term historical information. The sacred almanac is the older of the two calendars and may have been used by the Olmecs. Detail about these matters is nearly endless; the interested reader is referred to Morley's classic treatment for more information (Morley et al. 1983).

Writing in Mesoamerica began as pictographs that blended into the symbolism of art. Phoneticism appeared in the Izapan period, and the La Mojarra stela is an excellent example. The Maya pushed writing to its logical end, which is the possibility of carrying an abstract message without an oral or pictorial supplement. Generations of scholars worked on the problems of decipherment, but it was Tatiana Proskouriakoff who led the break-in to the Maya code. In a series of brilliant papers that began in 1960, she demonstrated the essential historicity of Maya texts on stone monuments (stelae). Yuri Knorozov had argued in the 1950s that Maya writing was phonetically based, but he was a voice in the wilderness. More recently, a group of younger scholars has demonstrated the validity of many of Knorozov's discoveries, leading the way into actual decipherment and translation of texts (e.g., Bricker 1986). The Maya wrote in an archaic form of Chol, one of the major lowland dialects, as well as in Yucatec, the dominant language of the Northern Lowlands. Much of the language is rhetorical, flowery, formal, and sometimes incomprehensible. Much of it has to do with rituals of accession, dynastic marriages, claims of conquest, and genealogies. Marcus (1992) has pointed out that much of this material is suspect because of the propaganda function of these records. However, as noted earlier, with care and cross-checking the materials can be used to supplement the archaeological record. This form of data gives us personality, much minor historical fluctuation, and dynastic records. Nearly seven hundred carved monuments are known, most from the Late Classic, and these are supplemented by tomb murals, wooden carvings, incised jades, and many texts on polychrome pottery. Unfortunately, many of the latter have been mercilessly looted from ancient tombs, and their contexts are unknown, and even their authenticity is suspect in some cases. Careful assessment of Rio Azul reveals that even with all the murals, sculptures, modeled stucco, polychrome pots, and other texts, less than 5 percent of the original total of written materials has survived (Robichaux 1990).

Thus the Maya Late Classic rulers presided over their various polities in pomp, circumstance, and apparent security. Huge numbers of people, perhaps twelve million at A.D. 800, toiled to maintain the cities and the aristocrats and to produce food enough for all. The elite part of society expanded during this period, probably from an Early Classic 5 percent fraction to 25 percent in the Late Classic. Immense swamp drainage projects were initiated for wetland gardening activities. Maya cities, large and small, existed in a carefully tended landscape with little of the wild jungle that we see today. The untamed tropical forests of recent centuries are a result of the catastrophe that overtook the Lowland Maya beginning about A.D. 840.

3

Mesoamerica:
Transformations and
the Late Civilizations

Catastrophe, Disasters, Recoveries, and Transformations

Of the major Classic civilizations of Mesoamerica, Teotihuacan appears to have been the first to fall. The first indications of difficulty for the empire and the great city were their withdrawal in the beginning of the 530s from the Maya Lowlands and from other long-distance trading partners to the southeast. This pullback was offset somewhat by expansion to the north and west, but these moves into the arid mining zones of the Gran Chichimeca did not really balance out the loss of commodities from the richer tropical zones. Internal stresses are reflected in increasing evidence for social inequalities. Considering these and other possible factors, however, Rene Millon accepts Cowgill's (1988:263) suggestion that bureaucratic inflexibility and interference may have brought the city down. Militarism appears to have been on the rise, and the political authority was shifting from a religiously sanctioned type to a more secular wielding of power (R. Millon 1988:146–149).

In any case, "the end of Teotihuacan as a major power was fiery and cataclysmic" (R. Millon 1988:149). About A.D. 650, temples, pyramids, palaces, and other public buildings were burned (53 percent), including nearly all of those located along the Street of the Dead. Fewer of the apartment compounds were burned (14 percent). The palaces of the Citadel were destroyed by fire and dismembered skeletons were found, some with shattered skulls. Millon says there was a certain excess in the destruction: "Temples, public buildings, and palaces were not merely destroyed—they were knocked down, torn apart, burned, reduced to rubble, time after time, building after building for more than two kilometers" (R. Millon 1988:153). Millon thinks that the ultimate aim was to destroy the symbols of power so thoroughly that there would be no possibility of recovery. Although Millon thinks that insiders did it, there is new evidence to suggest that it may have been done by military groups from the lowlands combined with internal dissidents.

Even after this disaster, Teotihuacan was still occupied by a substantial number of people, an estimated forty thousand, but it was no longer the political and religious center for the valley or the Central Highlands. Much of its population had dispersed into new and established cities in the central and southern Basin of Mexico. These populations carried on the traditions of Teotihuacan and invented new means of governance and new ways of looking at the world (see Map 3.1).

The two sites of Cacaxtla and Xochicalco might indicate that mercenary and opportunist military groups had penetrated the highlands just before the fall of Teotihuacan at about A.D. 650. However, both cities were established only after the catastrophe. At both sites there is art that indicates a hybrid mixture of cultures from highlands and Gulf Coast lowlands.

Cacaxtla is nearer Teotihuacan, strategically located between it and the Gulf Coast, and is fortified. Ten very large platforms each sustained palace complexes that may have housed not only the elite but their retainers as well in the manner so well attested by similar European and Chinese establishments. The defenses consist of the location on a hilltop, which is backed up by massive moats and possibly by parapets. Excavation of one palace has produced spectacular murals that show a battle between people from the lowlands and highlands. Although details and precise meanings are obscure, the art is a mixture of styles from both areas. Garcia-Cook (1981) thinks that the center was the capital of a group called the Olmeca-Xicalanca in later chronicles, who dominated the eastern highlands for about 350 years. The names are those of groups from the Gulf Coast, which therefore fits with the idea of intrusive military groups into the highlands at this time.

It is possible to draw a parallel with the Old World mercenaries, called *condottieri* in medieval Italy. These soldiers-for-hire sometimes worked for themselves and on occasion even set themselves up as legitimate rulers. The Sforzas of Milan are the most prominent case. In Mesoamer-

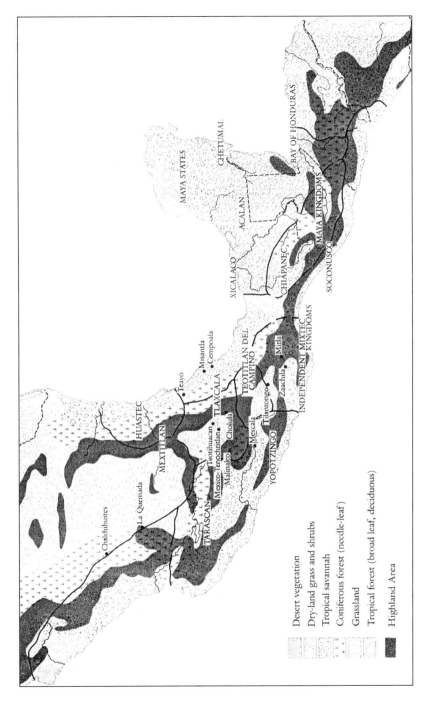

MAP 3.1 Postclassic Mesoamerica, showing principal sites mentioned in this chapter

ica, mercenaries were in common use by the A.D. 1100s. It seems entirely possible that they were in existence much earlier. If the people of Teotihuacan suffered from the same drastic shift as the Lowland Maya, in the 530s and later, then they faced massive famine and probably epidemic diseases at home. This would produce a weakened state, one whose manpower could not necessarily handle all its needs. The Gulf Coast zone was one that Teotihuacan had dominated and that produced formidable soldiers later. Therefore it seems entirely plausible that mercenaries from that area in the employ of Teotihuacan should turn on that state when it weakened and establish themselves as independent operators. The fall of the city may have been brought about by this combination of outside military pressure and internal weaknesses, as mentioned earlier. At that point, the former mercenaries were free to establish their own administrative centers and expand their states over as much area as they could manage. This would explain Cacaxtla early and Xochicalco later.

Xochicalco, which is located west and south of the Basin of Mexico, was also founded about A.D. 650. There had been substantial population in the area before this but only minor administrative centers and no major urban complex, according to Kenneth Hirth (1984). The fortified city was built after the fall of Teotihuacan and covered a series of adjacent hills with a total area of about 3.8 km² (1.5 mi²). Five concentric terrace walls fortified the city, and a road net tied the various segments of the city together, as is clear from Hirth's map (1984). The city flourished in spite of a remarkably arid and sparse environment and by A.D. 800 probably had a population of about fifteen thousand. It was undoubtedly sustained by tribute from other areas as well as by its own immediate resources. The topmost urban ring is on the summit of one of the hills and was closed to common access. An extensive palace, a very large temple, and several public buildings were placed there. The temple shows once again the hybrid art style that is derived from the Gulf Coast and Central Highlands. Three stelae in front of the temple depict Quetzalcoatl, the Feathered Serpent deity, but in Gulf Coast style. The writing and numerical style is distinctive and is largely pictographic. A series of sculpted plaques adorns the upper part of the main temple. Hirth (1995) has recently read these as records of conquest, naming twenty-six subjugated rulers and their capitals. A very large ball court located on the fourth terraced level is of the pattern used by the later Aztecs, and presumably the rules of the game were similar. There is much else of interest in the city, including drainage systems and paved walkways. Suffice it to say that this is another possible case of a mercenary military group intruding into the highlands and establishing itself as an elite over a mass of native population.

This, then, was the political pattern after the demise of Teotihuacan and its unifying influence. Elites, either native or foreign, established themselves and carved out regional states that were often hybrid versions of older cultural traditions. Emphasis on overt militarism was much more apparent than in Teotihuacan, and it is thought that more secularized rulership was also characteristic. This politically fragmented situation continued until the rise of another conquest state, which expanded to an imperial scale.

Late Classic Maya Civilization
and the Great Collapse

A long, successful, extraordinary series of florescences marked the course of Maya prehistory from 500 B.C. to A.D. 840. However, the Maya were ultimately exhausted by this effort and especially by the Late Classic tour de force of building, population expansion, and elite class demands. The explanation of the Maya collapse is now reasonably well understood, except by writers who still try to lure readers by the phrase "mysterious Maya." An explanation worked out at a 1970 conference, refined periodically since then, and bolstered by massive amounts of data is available in both technical and popular versions (Culbert 1973, 1974; Lowe 1985; Adams 1991). A short, clarified version is given here. The explanation revolves around the premise that the cause of the Maya downfall was not one factor but a number of interactive ingredients. The operations of these factors brought the Maya into a state of vulnerability, and when a triggering event occurred, an irreversible collapse followed.

The always-present element of population growth was an essential part of the disaster. It will be recalled that the Late Classic Maya experienced a population growth surge beginning about A.D. 650 and lasting for nearly two hundred years. This surge produced a landscape full of large and small cities embedded in rural aristocratic estates, farmsteads, and the full resources of an agricultural system that had developed every possibility. The periodic swamps (shallow depressions that fill with rainwater during the annual monsoon season) that occupy up to 40 percent of the area were converted to large expanses of wetland gardens. By means of drainage and huge numbers of raised fields, the depressions became productive areas. Floodland cultivation, slash-and-burn, and short-term fallow systems were among those that the Maya used to produce food for hundreds of thousands of people. It appears that it was not sufficient. Late Classic skeletons from elite as well as commoner burials show progressive deterioration of health status. As a result of increasingly poor diets that relied on more carbohydrates and ever smaller amounts of animal and vegetable proteins, the Maya experienced a number of problems (Saul 1973). Their average height dropped, and diseases due to malnutrition, such as scurvy and severe forms of anemia, became increasingly common. Children's teeth frequently show horizontal lines that are marks of growth interruption due to severe fasting. The homeland of the Maya is also one of tropical diseases such as a New World form of malaria, yellow fever, and Chagas' disease. The latter causes cardiac problems and early death due to a blood parasite. A New World form of syphilis seems to have been present. These and other maladies were endemic. Although the Maya knew a great amount about herbal medicines and their healing potential, these techniques were not sufficient to deal with major outbreaks of disease due to malnutrition caused, say, by crop failures. There is no evidence of any form or concept of public health among the Maya, nor indeed anywhere else in the world until the eighteenth century. Widespread and increasingly large tropical zone irrigation systems even today allow the development and rapid spread of viruses. Large amounts of standing water in ditches, combined with poor sanitation, inevitably lead to polluted water and lethal health hazards. The large cities produced huge amounts of human waste; one adult produces about a pound of solid waste per day, and Tikal had a population of eighty thousand. The food production systems themselves created ecological problems in the form of water loss and soil erosion.

Expansion of the total population was accompanied by an increase in the size of the elite, none of whom were food producers, but all of whom consumed a disproportionate amount of resources. The ruling classes also demanded luxuries that had to be produced by full-time artisans or imported by long-distance trade, both costly in terms of time and absorption of valuable personnel. The aristocrats also were characteristically contentious and sparked wars between cities and regional states over political ambitions as well as over matters of pride and vanity. Warfare is a notoriously wasteful and expensive enterprise, and it became more frequent as time went on. In the final stages of the collapse warfare became the last recourse of desperate people trying to take scarce resources from their equally stricken neighbors. This was particularly the case between the northern Yucatec Maya and the southern Maya. There are at least five well-documented cases of military predation from north to south in the final part of the Late Classic.

The trigger bringing about the catastrophic collapse of Maya cultural systems was a long-term drought that set in at about A.D. 840 and broke down the food production systems for lack of water (Gill 1994). Owing to a very complex set of interrelated weather systems, cooling in the northern part of the Northern Hemisphere does not reach the Maya area until about fifteen years later. This means that ancient climates can be reconstructed for the Maya with the help of Greenland ice cores, North Atlantic sea cores, and other data such as lake and pond varves. These convincingly show a cool, dry trend at a slightly earlier time than the onset of the Maya drought. The ultimate trigger may have been another extremely violent volcanic eruption, perhaps even from El Chichón. What is certain is that the effects were devastating. In any given Lowland Maya region the sequence of disaster was probably different. However, we know that both nobility and commoners went down together. The population loss was at least 85 percent. The cities and the countryside were deserted in a short time, perhaps as long as seventy-five years but maybe as short as twenty-five. All social, political, and economic systems broke down. Food shortages caused famines and, very rapidly, epidemics. In the case of Tikal, the aristocrats appear to have been buffered against the initial effects but then were deprived of their supporting population and their remnants left to fend for themselves among the deteriorating palaces and temples. In some zones, military intruders accelerated the collapse, but this was a symptom of weakness, not the ultimate cause of the breakdown. At Rio Azul, a northern military raid, probably from the Uxmal vicinity, came in and destroyed the city again. The aristocrats who took refuge in the nearby fortress of Kinal survived, but this simply was a matter of putting off the inevitable. As around Tikal, the exhausted farmlands rapidly went back to second growth and eventually to recovery forest. Tikal's old rival, Calakmul, went down in much the same way, and without people to maintain them, trees began to grow in the great plazas and on the magnificent buildings. Vaulted roofs probably began to collapse within fifty years, and by A.D. 900 many structures were well into the process of disintegration. Most of the tropical zone occupied by the Classic Maya has not been inhabited for eleven hundred years. Only under the twentieth-century pressures of population growth have Mexican and Guatemalan people moved back into the area.

Comparisons

The Maya collapse is nearly unique in world history in that it was a catastrophe from which there was no cultural or demographic recovery. Most political/cultural disasters have survivors, many of them, who rebuild their cultural systems in new and more adaptive forms. The breakdowns of Teotihuacan and Monte Alban were of this kind. The German catastrophe in World War II is a more recent example. For the Maya, however, there was no comeback. Some instructive historical partial parallels to the Maya case should be mentioned. In 1348, Europe was in a state of vulnerability similar to that of the Late Classic Maya as a result of human populations' having outgrown the current food production systems. Plagues had affected cattle, sheep, and other livestock, and crop failures had occurred in the immediately preceding years. Peasants were forced to cultivate clayey soils that had never before (and never since) been cultivated, in the Bordeaux region of France, for example. With increasingly fragile health status, a marginal food supply, and an archaic form of distribution, the literal death blow was struck by the introduction of bubonic and pneumonic plagues. The effects were immediate: for example, Zurich lost 60 percent of its population in the summer of 1348. Moreover, for the next 150 years periodic plagues swept Europe and, in the opinion of some historians, destroyed the old organization of medieval society. Of course, in the European case, there was a recovery, and it was the brilliant period known as the Renaissance (Adams and Smith 1977).

The Club of Rome Model

Finally, we should refer to a *predictive* model of present-day trends that have strikingly close parallels to the actual Maya occurrence. T. P. Culbert first pointed out these similarities in 1974. The Club of Rome, a group of Italian intellectuals and industrialists worried about exponential growth rates in world populations, commissioned a computer simulation in the late 1960s. The aim of the study was to determine what would happen, and when, if the rates of growth in population, industrialization, food production, pollution, and use of nonrenewable resources continued. Note that all the factors are interactive. The conclusions were that if all factors of exponential growth were not controlled, the modern world faced global catastrophes on an unprecedented scale beginning about the year A.D. 2000 (Meadows et al. 1972). Criticism of the model largely focused on a statistical error, but correction of the error simply has the effect of delaying the onset of disasters for a generation or less. A recent restudy by the same group has concluded that twenty years after the first publication of the model, the progress toward catastrophe is unfortunately on track and on schedule. Let us now turn from these apocalyptic visions to the transformed cultures of the Mesoamerican Postclassic period.

El Tajin: A Transitional Regional Civilization

On the northern Gulf Coast, near the present-day town of Papantla, lie the ruins of a city strikingly different in its architecture from those previously discussed. Although there were numerous small towns and villages in the vicinity before A.D. 550, none achieved the status of a city. El Tajin was a relatively minor administrative center during the great period of Teotihuacan. After the withdrawal of Teotihuacan, El Tajin burgeoned into a magnificent city that was the capital of a regional state that spread south along the coast. In this area of perennial rivers and heavy rainfall, the effects of the global climatic deterioration of A.D. 534 to 600 seem to have been ameliorated. At any rate, the regional culture flourished from A.D. 500 to 1100. The city grew to cover an area of approximately 5 km² (nearly 2 mi²), with at least 3,500 people in the urban center and an estimated 13,000 in the vicinity (Krotser and Krotser 1973; Wilkerson 1987:73). Hills and a small valley are the setting for a number of courtyard groups with temples, palaces, and eleven ball courts all in a distinctive local style. A very large pyramid with 365 niches in it was presumably dedicated to the solar year in some manner. Sculpture covers tablets on temples and ball courts, and the subject matter is heavy with human sacrifice. Maguey (century) plants are watered with sacrificial blood, and hieroglyphs refer insistently to a certain 13 Rabbit, who was probably the greatest ruler of the city and the state. Warfare, human sacrifice, and conquest for tribute—all are themes that presage the aggressive and more secularized cultures of Mesoamerica from about A.D. 1000 onward. El Tajin, Cacaxtla, and Xochicalco are early and transitional cultures that led to that dominant pattern.

There are a number of other cultures of this category and period, but they are only fragmentarily known. Cholula, in the east central highlands, is one of these; apparently it arose in tandem with Cacaxtla not far away. However, the site is heavily overlain with sixteenth-century, colonial, and

modern architecture and not much detail is known. On the periphery of
Mesoamerica, however, 64 km (40 miles) to the north of the Valley of
Mexico, still another regional center was established and growing that be-
came the capital of the next empire of the Central Highlands.

Tula and the Toltecs

Very many were the marvelous houses which they made. The house of
Quetzalcoatl, which was his place of worship, stood in the water; a large
river passed by it; the river which passed by Tula. . . . Many houses stood
within the earth where the Tolteca left many things buried.

Sahagun, The Florentine Codex, 1961 (Book 10)

Tollan, or Place of the Reeds, is the original name of the Toltec capital at
Tula. Although north of the Basin of Mexico, the zone was known in ancient times as The Land of the Gods. There is good evidence that it was a
fertile, favorable place in which to live, with forests and streams. It was in
this setting that a small administrative center was established by Teotihuacan. However, after A.D. 650 it was on its own and became politically
independent. At some point the Toltecs chose the center for their capital,
probably by A.D. 800, and within the next two hundred years it grew to
cover an area of ca. 14 km² (5.4 mi²) with about thirty-five thousand inhabitants. The city is laid out around the confluence of two rivers, a
marshy zone, and surrounding hills. On the nose of a ridge, the major
temples, palaces, and ball court are laid out and fortified with steep stone-
faced terraces as much as 18 m (60 feet) high. The elite precinct is divided
from the rest of the city by a stone wall. The very battered remains of
three major temples are oriented around the main plaza. One of these
buildings is decorated with carved stone panels depicting prowling jaguars
and eagles, some grasping human hearts in their paws and claws. Atop the
platform was once a temple; enormous Atlantean figures supported the
roof. A great colonnade runs along the front of the temple, and a three-
courtyard palace is also behind the forest of columns. The interest here is
not merely in the detail of the structure but in the fact that it is a very
close duplicate of one at the northern Maya city of Chichen Itza, about
which more later. A very large ball court is laid out in the shape of a capi-

tal I. Although impressive in concept and in architectural realization, the buildings were shabbily constructed. Large timber columns were incorporated into stone walls, making the buildings exceedingly flammable and a fire marshal's nightmare. All indications point to hasty and slapdash work.

Whatever their failings in a material sense, however, the Toltecs developed a new and virulent ideology that came down to the Aztecs in a slightly modified version. This was the concept of the "sacred war" in which mankind was obligated to aid the gods, and especially the sun, in their continual struggle with the powers of darkness. Part of the help required was in the form of worship that increasingly revolved around human sacrifice and offerings of other kinds as well. A conquest-state mentality is evident in the symbolism at Tula. The eagles and jaguars are the symbols of the day and night sun. The eagle represented the sun in its daily flight through the sky and the jaguar the sun in its nightly journey through the caverns of the earth from west to east. Later Aztec elite warrior societies were associated with these manifestations of the sun and were especially committed to the capture of sacrificial victims through war. Therefore, although war carried the practical aspects of economic gain and slave labor, it also assumed a divine quality through these linkages.

Along the gentler, wider slopes and tops of the same ridge as well as down in the valley were dozens of house compounds made of adobe bricks with flat roofs. At first glance, these residences resemble nothing so much as the peasant homes of traditional Mexicans. In fact, Diehl and his colleagues think that the houses were homes for extended families, with two or more generations living together in house clusters (Diehl 1983; Healan 1974). Most of the thirty-five thousand citizens of Tula resided in such house compounds. According to the chronicles, there were also foreign ethnic groups residing in the city.

The Ethnohistoric Record

The archaeological record begins to mesh with the remnants of prehistoric chronicles at about A.D. 1000. The histories kept by later peoples of the Valley of Mexico were partly translated into Latin script after the Spanish conquest and have reached us in partial and sometimes corrupted versions. With care, as with the deciphered native texts, one can use these to supplement the culture histories and theories of archaeology. As with all historical records, one must evaluate them as to authenticity, motivation for writing, the perspective of the author(s), and reliability. The chronicles that

mention the Toltecs are heavily dynastic histories as well as allegorical re-
countings of mythical and real events. A list of Toltec rulers, which is apparently historical, runs from a queen who appeared about A.D. 829 to the
last ruler, Huemac, who disposed of himself in A.D. 1162. The great Mexican historian Wigberto Jimenez-Moreno has studied and reconciled the
various Toltec accounts, and this section relies on his synthesis (1966). The
fall of Teotihuacan brought the Toltecs into the Valley of Mexico, and they
settled in a lakeside city, Ixtapalapa, where they stayed for some generations. They left the Valley of Mexico to escape the Olmec tyranny as exercised from Cholula and went to Tula to establish their capital. A certain
ruler, Topiltzin, also known as Quetzalcoatl, led the move, possibly at A.D.
960 (which seems very late). At any rate, once there Quetzalcoatl became
embroiled in a power struggle with a political/religious faction who es-
poused the worship of Tezcatlipoca. According to the chronicles, Quetzalcoatl detested human sacrifice and urged the offering of flowers, fruits, and
some animals. Tezcatlipoca, the lord of darkness, on the other hand, pro-
moted human sacrifice and all of the horrors that went with it. Quetzalcoatl was defeated through trickery and left Tula with his followers. The
group underwent a long migration, arriving in Yucatan at one point. Finally, Quetzalcoatl became discouraged and sailed off into the rising sun,
promising to return or send his sons to reclaim his patrimony. This myth
captured the imagination of the Mesoamericans and, as will be seen, had a
significant historical effect in later Aztec times. Tula fell in about A.D.
1156; Huemac transferred the capital to Chapultepec in the Valley of
Mexico and died there in 1162. Later Mesoamericans had wholehearted
admiration for the Toltecs and looked back upon their time as a kind of
golden age. Ruling houses of later periods attempted to legitimize themselves by tracing their ancestry to a Toltec origin.

The Consequences of Long-Distance Trade

Considerable evidence for contact with many zones of Mesoamerica has
come from work at Tula, some in the form of ceramics from the Pacific
coast of Guatemala (Plumbate ware), from Costa Rica (Nicoya Polychrome), and from the southernmost Gulf Coast area (Fine Orange).
These and other materials were imported to Tula, which seems to have
been the center of a vast trading network through which many traditional
and new items were distributed. Judging by the practices of the later
Aztecs, the Tula Toltecs probably sent out state-supported trading expedi-

tions. One notable new set of skills and commodities that spread throughout Mesoamerica was metallurgy, which had been introduced from Central or South America about A.D. 800. None of this new technology was applied practically, however, and most of the metals used were soft, such as copper, gold, and silver. The principal items made of metal were jewelry for the elite, religious paraphernalia, and elite commemorations.

It was at this time that the Toltecs made a notable contact with the vast area of present-day northern Mexico and the southwestern United States. A series of small and large centers had earlier and gradually developed on the basis of long-distance trade in commodities available from these regions: exotic stones, mercury and cinnabar, and the like. The Toltecs drove this development to its logical extension—a chain of communities from south to north along the inside edge of the western Sierra Madre. Eventually the route reached the Hohokam culture of southern Arizona and the Anasazi in the Chaco Canyon region. Northern Mexican centers like Casas Grandes (DiPeso 1974) facilitated the passage of the merchants, providing safety, rest, and supplies. They also traded on their own account. For example, people in Casas Grandes (the ancient Paquime) raised macaws and traded their brilliantly colored feathers north, possibly for turquoise and copper.

A number of significant cultural traits were introduced into Anasazi and Hohokam cultures. The Mesoamerican ball game was played on a capital I-shaped court at a large center now near the modern city of Phoenix. Miraculously, an actual imported rubber ball was found, although after about nine hundred years it lacked much bounce (Haury 1937). The traditional Kachina dancers of the Rio Grande pueblos may be derived from a rain god cult introduced from Mesoamerica. A colonnaded forecourt, similar to that of Tula Structure B, was found in Chaco Canyon. A number of other traits may derive from the influence of resident and visiting Mesoamericans, but these were assimilated selectively and on the terms of the native cultures. No evidence for human sacrifice is known, for example, and apparently the Anasazi and Hohokam were not interested in the associated concept of divine war. In other areas of Mesoamerica, however, the Toltec presence and influence were much less benign.

The Toltec Invasion of Yucatan

While the collapse in the central and southern Maya Lowlands was underway, the northern peninsula maintained itself, partly through raids on the increasingly vulnerable south. A major regional state in northeastern Yucatan was headed by the city of Coba, and another in the northwest had its capital at Uxmal. The Coba Regional State was successful for a long time and physically tied itself with its tributary cities by means of an extensive road network. The roads were actually causeways elevated as much as 3 m (10 feet) above the landscape; they were as much as 18 m (60 feet) wide. They appear to have been designed for use by trains of porters transporting goods at night. The white paved surfaces would have been visible in those cooler hours, making traveling easier. Military use was undoubtedly a consideration. The Coba Regional State appears to have gone under from many of the same conditions as those that afflicted the southern cities and states and at about the same time. The Puuc (Uxmal) Regional State, however, appears to have flourished during the southern collapse and outlasted that disaster until about A.D. 1000.

The Puuc Hills of Yucatan are a set of low ridges located just about 89 air km (55 air miles) to the south of the Caribbean Sea. In this area, a long Preclassic buildup had gone through the evolutionary stages needed to produce state-level societies by about 250 B.C., but the polities remained small until the Late Classic. After about A.D. 800, population began to grow dramatically, and several centers became very large cities, especially Uxmal and its linked subordinates such as Kabah and Labna. As mentioned in the section "Late Classic Maya Civilization and the Great Collapse," the northern cities, especially Uxmal, raided into the south and probably regarded the agricultural labor there as one of the treasures to be looted. The buildup of population in the Puuc seems too rapid and sudden to account for it by internal growth. The construction of the magnificent cities of the Puuc required skilled workmen, also available in the southern states. Uxmal therefore may have expanded and lived on the accumulated skills of captive southern populations. A fortification wall around Uxmal (only recently mapped) is another indication of the residents' interest in warfare. The northern Maya were quite different from the southern regional states in that their elites had accepted the ideology and symbols of the "divine war," probably from central Mexico. Because of the intense canoe traffic around the peninsula and the salt/honey trade from the north, there would be every opportunity to meet such ideas and adopt them. At any rate, eagles—the Central Mexican sun symbols—appear on the facades of late Uxmal temples. An indigenous interest in phallicism is strong at Uxmal and other Puuc sites, with a gigantic example located in front of the primary palace (the Palace of the Governor) and a group of such sculptures presently located just off the platform of the same structure. Rain god masks were incorporated into the facades of formal buildings in prominent positions, and one building at Kabah is completely covered with such masks.

Chichen Itza, located about 135 km (85 miles) east-northeast of Uxmal, was a subordinate center for the Puuc Regional State. Rain god masks and very large palaces were built in the Late Classic period, although Chichen appears to have been unfortified. At some point, not precisely known, the Toltec of Central Mexico appeared and conquered Yucatan. Uxmal and its regional state collapsed, but the details are unknown, thanks to some of the most poorly done archaeology in Mesoamerica. Although all of the foregoing is reasonably certain, the material in the following section is somewhat speculative.

A Reconstruction of the Toltec Conquest

The following is derived somewhat from J. W. Ball's study of events in the northern Maya Lowlands (1985). The Itza were a Maya group from the southern Tabasco plain, and not one of the major players in the Classic period. They apparently came into Yucatan as allies of the Toltec, who themselves may have been mercenaries working for Uxmal. The two allies apparently picked off the outlying Puuc centers and then Uxmal. They were able to prevail because of superior tactics and the extensive use of the bow and arrow, a weapon for some reason never favored by the Classic Maya. Scenes of the conquest of Yucatan are found in profusion at Chichen, sculpted on columns and door jambs, painted on walls in mural form, and hammered into magnificent gold plaques. There are a number of scenes of Toltec canoe raids on Maya communities and others showing houses afire, siege towers in operation against walled towns, rampant Toltec warriors everywhere triumphing over abased and defeated Maya, and human sacrifices of prisoners. The Puuc was devastated; water storage systems fell into ruin and disuse, and the cities of the Maya were once more abandoned to the reviving jungle. Thus the collapse of the late northern Maya cities was a more nearly "standard" military/political disaster with the survivors incorporated into a new regime. The Toltecs established their colonial administrative center at Chichen by A.D. 987 and built an extraordinary set of buildings in a style that was a mixture of Toltec and Puuc.

Toltec Chichen Itza

Consulting a map of the Yucatan peninsula, one can see why the Toltecs chose to locate their chief administrative center at Chichen. It was roughly in the center of the northern plain and near the coast, but not so near as to be subject to raids from the sea or to hurricanes. Further, it was a long-standing center of religious pilgrimage and a huge sinkhole (*cenote*) was the focus of a rain god cult. A final consideration was that major salt fields are spread along the coast north of Chichen. Thus the sacred, political, military, and economic factors combined to make the center a well-located colonial capital.

The "sacred *cenote*" is an impressive hole in the bedrock measuring about 60 m (190 feet) across, with 24 m (80 feet) of sheer drop to the water and then another 12 m (40 feet) of water to the bottom. Objects dredged from the well date from about 800 B.C. to A.D 1550 and come from all over Mesoamerica and from beyond its boundaries (Coggins 1992). Human victims were also thrown into the well; mainly young males and deformed persons. Another large sinkhole with the water table exposed was used for the city's water supply. The Toltecs linked the sacred well to their most imposing temple, dedicated to Quetzalcoatl, or Kukulcan (feathered serpent) in Maya. This temple and the Temple of the Warriors were built and rebuilt in at least one major renovation, indicating a long period of occupation, perhaps for two hundred years according to the Maya chronicles. The platform of the Temple of the Warriors is a near replica of the basal platform of Structure B at Tula. Similar motifs are placed in similar recessed panels of sculpture running in bands around the structure. The temples were quite different, however. At Chichen the roof was supported by square columns carved with the portraits of Toltec warriors (the officers?), and the doorway is flanked by two giant rattlesnakes stiffened into columns. The colonnaded forecourt is the same in concept, but again the thousand columns at Chichen are carved on all four sides with the stiff portraits of warriors (the enlisted men?). The ball court is the largest and most grandiose in Mesoamerica and decorated with scenes of conquest, human sacrifice, and other grim motifs. Measured against the sophistication and general delicacy of Classic Maya art, this body of depictions is relatively crude, unimaginative, and mechanical.

Among the buildings of the period at Chichen are some low platforms that reflect the new concepts of the universe and that of "sacred war." These platforms are decorated with carved panels on their sides. One set of decorations emphasizes eagles and jaguars, which gloat over human hearts. Another is more explicit and shows human skulls impaled on stakes and strung on a wooden rack. Because the Aztecs followed the same practice, we can identify this platform as the Toltec tzompantli, or display rack for the skulls of sacrificial victims. Presumably an actual rack was mounted on the platform. The other platforms, including a very large one on the way to the sacred cenote, were for public ceremonies, which probably included human sacrifice. Clearly the Maya had been incorporated into a new ideological and social order, one that emphasized military leadership and the terrifying rites of offering human beings to the gods.

The Itza, who gave their name to the city, were probably surrogate rulers for the Toltecs, but there was no doubt who held the power. By two hundred years after the conquest, however, the Itza were probably more Maya than the Yucatec. After 1156, Tula was gone and Chichen was on its own and probably had been for some time. By A.D. 1187 the Toltec episode was over in Yucatan, and after losing out in political intrigues the descendants of the Itza moved south into the lake district of northern Guatemala and settled on the peninsula and island of Tayasal.

Late Maya Civilizations

Hunac Ceel, the ruler of a small city in northeastern Yucatan, intervened in a conflict between the rulers of Chichen and those of another city, turned on both of them, and unified the Northern Lowlands. The previously insignificant city of Mayapan became the capital of this Maya regional state from A.D. 1250 until 1446. Political control and order were achieved by the requirement that members of the ruling houses of Yucatan reside in Mayapan. Their stewards arranged for their support from their native provinces, according to the native chronicles studied by Ralph Roys (1962). All went well for several generations, and the ruling family of Cocoms maintained their superior status until a late ruler brought in Mexican mercenaries to ensure security. A conspiracy then developed among the disenfranchised nobility that exploded with a massacre of the Cocoms, destruction of their palaces and the civic center, and the abandonment of the city. The remains of the city are unimpressive, but they have been well studied. The city is surrounded by a medium-sized wall that may have been topped with a wooden palisade. Several gates give entrance to the city, which covers an area of 3.8 km² (1.5 mi²). The majority of the 4,140 structures inside the wall were houses or auxiliary buildings. An estimated twelve thousand people lived at Mayapan, most of them aristocrats or servants and retainers associated with such households. No avenues lead to the administrative and religious center, and house lot walls confine the visitor to narrow alleys. The 121 major temples, administrative buildings, and palaces of the city were mainly grouped into a single complex. Some buildings are pale copies of those at Toltec Chichen: a smaller temple to Kukulcan, for example, but in the same style. Quetzalcoatl, or Kukulcan, was said to be the founder of the city, but this must have been a pretense to mythical antiquity and prestige. Unlike earlier Maya capitals, Mayapan lacked a ball court and did not carry over the skull rack (tzompantli) from Toltec Chichen. The rulers did invest heavily in the prestige of twenty-five carved and painted stone monuments (stelae), a long-standing Maya tradition. Mayapan was remarkable for its political unification of the northern peninsula, not for its monumental remains; those were things of the past. In fact, if we had no chronicle histories for the episode, it might be difficult to reconstruct what actually had happened.

The end at Mayapan is archaeologically plain; the city and its buildings were torn apart and, as in the case of Teotihuacan earlier, an effort was made to destroy all symbols of the political power that had held the noble families virtually captive. The League of Mayapan broke apart into its constituent parts, and no doubt considerable adjustment of provincial borders and jostling among the independent states took place over the next seventy years. By 1519, when Cortez visited the Northern Lowlands, the area was divided into sixteen regional states. Three kinds of government were in place, ranging from a single ruler (Halach Uinic) to a council of town governors *(batabs)* allied through kinship and an even more loosely grouped set of governors bound by common tradition and proximity (Roys 1957:6–7). The Regional State of Mani was one of the most important and included a lot of the old territory of the Puuc Regional State from the Classic period. The Tutul-Xiu, who were the ruling family, resided in the capital town of Mani. They had briefly occupied the old Puuc capital of Uxmal but moved to Mani after the fall of Mayapan. They became valuable allies of the Spaniards in the conquest after 1542 (Roys 1957:61–64).

Another province, Chikinchel or Chauaca, exploited its location on the central north coast to produce huge amounts of salt, which it exported via the canoe traffic around the peninsula. Something like 3,008,000 liters (85,000 bushels) of salt were sent out each year along with copal (incense), another commodity much in demand. The language and intellectual achievements of the inhabitants of Chikinchel were looked upon by the rest of the Maya as the most refined of any in the Northern Lowlands. This regional state was one ruled by a council of *batabs*.

By the sixteenth century the lowland Maya aristocrats had adapted themselves to the new conditions and were, in essence, merchant princes. Tulum, a small city on the east coast of Yucatan that is now much visited by tourists, was heavily involved in trade from Central America to the Gulf Coast. Two of its principal exports were probably honey and beeswax (sugarcane and sugar beets are native to the Old World, but not the New, and thus a principal pre-Hispanic sweetening agent was honey). Images of the bee gods—the so-called diving gods—are found over the doorways of some Tulum buildings. The nearby island of Cozumel was the shrine of the moon goddess and was a goal of pilgrims. Navigational aids in the form of small shrines, which were probably light-houses of a sort, are located all up and down the coast in this area.

A few Maya in the Southern Lowlands survived the ninth-century catastrophe and settled on the lakes in the Peten, the northern district in Guatemala. There, the Itza rulers came from the north and ruled until 1697, the last native civilization in the New World. They continued their traditions of rulership, of religious worship of numerous gods, and of writing and mathematics. All of these and the native state were overthrown in a one-day battle when the Spanish finally subjugated these people as they had all the rest of the Mesoamericans.

Zapotecs and Mixtecs in Oaxaca

The abandonment of Monte Alban appears to have been gradual and related to the fall of Teotihuacan. During the Classic period, the continued growth of Monte Alban appears to have been partially a defense against a threat from Teotihuacan. With the disappearance of this menace, the logistical problems of maintaining a large population on a relatively sterile ridge caused the city to lose its purpose. However, even in the late pre-Hispanic period, Monte Alban had a substantial population of about six thousand (Blanton 1983:282). From about A.D. 600 to 900, there was a scramble for power among the noble families who had once made up the ruling oligarchy at the great capital city (Flannery and Marcus 1983:183–185). Groups of these families established themselves at centers located in the open valley bottom lands and were supported by retainer commoner families. Lambityeco was one of these centers; it is located in the eastern arm of the valley. Small palace complexes and patio groups dispersed over the landscape are typical, and as in the Maya Lowlands, closely packed urban centers became few and far between. Marcus also notes a change in the nature of the stone monuments that emphasized genealogical registers and marriage alliances among elite families (Marcus 1983:191–197). Nearby Yagul was built in this period and consists of defensible palaces, a ball court, and a citadel on a butte. Perhaps it became a refuge for the ruling families in the increasingly unsettled times from A.D. 800 onward. The fortified town of Mitla is an extraordinary center a few miles east of Yagul. Mitla was about 2.59 km² (about 1 mi²), with huge and elaborately decorated palaces. These famous structures carry elaborate running frets and other geometric mosaics in their walls. These mosaics are general religious symbols of the elements of the universe. The buildings were also once decorated by murals in codex style; that is, the same scribal style found in the surviving books of the Zapotec. The structures are arranged around courtyards under which were formal tombs. We are told by a Spanish chronicler that this particular center was a traditional burial place for Zapotec priests (Paddock 1966). It was also the center for the worship of the lords of the underworld.

The rival Mixtecs were pressing on the Zapotecs by A.D. 800, and it is possible that the fall of Teotihuacan allowed the Mixtecs to expand into what had previously been Zapotec territory. This expansion picked up after A.D. 900 and is recorded in many of the surviving historical codices of the Mixtec. Not all expansion was at the expense of the Zapotec, for the Mixtec nobility were perfectly willing to subjugate neighboring Mixtecs if opportunity offered. In fact, the Postclassic nobility (post–A.D. 900) were largely free of attachment to a region and even to ethnic or linguistic groups. The generalized feudal system that had developed meant, among other things, that the landless commoners owed absolute fealty to their lords and went with them on their military and political adventures.

Many Mixtec codices carry accounts of multiple royal marriages, conquests, territories belonging to kingdoms and lords, and associated information. One notable account is of a famous ruler named 8 Deer Tiger Claw, who lived from A.D. 1011 to 1063. At the age of nineteen he succeeded to power when his father died. He used one of the towns left him by his father as a base for conquest and built up, by this means and by multiple marriages (five), a kingdom that may have been the largest ever created in the Mixteca region in this last phase of the pre-Hispanic period. He made a trip to Tula and there was invested with the sign of a legitimate ruler, a jade ornament pierced through the septum of his nose. When he was fifty-two, his judgment failed him, and he attacked the town of some of his in-laws, who promptly defeated and sacrificed him as is graphically shown in Codex Bodley (Flannery and Marcus 1983:218–219). These and other events of the life of 8 Deer were more or less standard in the lives of Mixtec and Zapotec rulers of the time, except for his extraordinary success and dismal end. Such incidents show the tactics, hazards, and continual problems of leading a small state, one usually at odds with other small states. This has been properly called a condition of balkanization. Fortified cities and centers became the norm during this last period of Oaxacan pre-history. These larger communities were supported by networks of tributary villages, towns, and even cities.

Several spectacular tombs from the period have been found. One at Za-achila was possibly of a ruler also mentioned in the codices. Beautifully made pottery, typical of the period and place, include a goblet with a blue bird perched on its edge, drinking. Monte Alban Tomb 7 dates from this period and contains an immense treasure trove of gold, silver, copper, carved bone, jade, and other materials. The treasure is in the form of ex-quisite workmanship as well as of intrinsically valuable materials. The principal buried in the tomb was a human monster with horrible congen-ital deformities, who perhaps was regarded as a deity in his lifetime. His obsequies were accompanied by the sacrifice of about nine adult males, two women, and one infant, all of whom presumably accompanied him into the afterworld. The style of the carved bones from the tomb indicates that it is that of a Mixtec rather than Zapotec (Marcus 1983:285).

The Mixtecs and Zapotecs united on occasion in spite of the history of warfare, intrigue, and double-dealing between them. One such occurrence was in 1497 when the Aztecs unsuccessfully besieged the fortress of Guiengola in Tehuantepec for seven months. The Zapotec ruler who led the resistance then bilked his Mixtec allies by allotting them very poor lands. In fact, as Marcus (1983c) points out, the Zapotec greatly preferred diplomacy to warfare, and if it were not possible to avoid the latter, they arranged to have the Mixtecs fight their major battles. However, matters did not always go well, and in 1521 the same ruler asked the Spanish for help against the Mixtec. The Spanish came and conquered both people in a short, brutal campaign.

The Tarascans of Western Mexico

Of all the peoples and languages of Mesoamerica, the Tarascans are the most enigmatic. For one thing, their language is distantly related to only two others in the New World, those of the Zuñi of New Mexico and the

Quechua of the Central Andes. Some contacts between Mesoamerica and South America are suggested by artifacts and events scattered through time and space. About 1500 B.C. for example, two parts of the west coast of Mexico produced pottery that is strikingly similar to contemporary material from coastal Ecuador and Peru. Metallurgy might have come from South America but as easily might have been imported from closer Central America, which had its own long tradition of metalworking. As noted earlier, this technology does not appear until A.D. 800 at the earliest and then diffuses mainly through Toltec trade networks. We cannot trace Tarascan origins back beyond A.D. 1000, and so all these bits of evidence are floating, disconnected, and unconvincing.

The fact is, however, that the Tarascans were different in a number of important way from other Mesoamericans, and the possibility remains that they were an intrusive military elite group who came into a relatively backwards area of Mesoamerica and made themselves the lords of all they could hold. Another possibility, of course, is that they came originally from what is now the southwestern United States and that is the reason for their linguistic tie with the Zuñi. These speculations aside, the Tarascans were successful empire builders and in some ways were more adept than the better-known Aztec.

The Tarascan empire in 1521 covered ca. 65,000 km² (about 25,000 mi²) but was largely a rural zone with only four cities worthy of the name. By far the largest and grandest was the city of Tzintzuntzan, which was also the capital. This place had been founded about A.D. 1000 as a religious center, but by A.D. 1350 it was an urban zone with a population of about thirty thousand people. A very large palace was located here as well as the ancestral tombs and very large temples of the rulers. At least five Tarascan temples were round in plan and set upon high and distinctively shaped platforms. The king was evidently a sacred person, and when he died, several retainers went with him into the afterlife. Rulers governed with the help of a council, presumably of great nobles. The main city was one of ethnic and occupational diversity with artisans organized into craft guilds. The Spanish chronicles mention bureaucrats, priests, storytellers, spies, couriers, and many other vocations. The three other cities were largely administrative and "summer palace" establishments. Most people lived in hamlets, towns, and villages: 335 of them. It will be recalled that the village way of life persisted in western Mexico into very late times and therefore, when the Tarascan elite appeared, there were few complex traditions to deal with. This situation allowed the development of a highly rationalized administrative structure that included professional soldiers (Gorenstein and Pollard 1983). This cadre of military specialists may account for the fact that the Aztecs had no success whatever against the Tarascans. Such a governmental structure and army are in high contrast to those of the Aztec, who largely relied on a well-trained but socially disparate militia as the basis for their armies (Hassig 1988:28–30). The government of the Aztecs was exceedingly complex, as will be seen, and derived partly from the long experience and varied traditions of the cultured peoples of the basin.

The Totonac of the Gulf Coast

On the humid, rich plains of what are now the states of Veracruz and Tabasco, the peoples of the tropical lowlands had undergone the vicissitudes and traumas normal to civilized societies of long standing. There is little doubt that by A.D. 1400 this area was inhabited by a linguistic and cultural group known as the Totonacs. Several major cities formed the nuclei of regional and smaller states that probably competed with one another in the normal Mesoamerican fashion. Large numbers of people were supported by irrigation and extensive wetland gardening as well as by trade and tribute. The Aztecs conquered this zone by 1472, perhaps motivated on the one hand by the unfailing bumper harvests of corn for which the region was famous and on the other hand by a series of disastrous crop failures of their own in the 1450s. In addition, control of this region gave the central highlanders access to the important canoe trade that reached around the Gulf and into the Caribbean. The details of Totonac history are obscure as a result of lack of excavation and scanty publication of the work that has been done. One of the major cities of Totonacapan (the Land of the Totonacs) was Cempoala. The civic precincts of the city have been exposed, but little culture history has been published. The temples, palaces, and civic structures cover a zone of at least 120,000 m² (ca. 30 acres). Informal survey has indicated that commoner housing was densely packed around the elite courtyards. On the basis of Spanish accounts, it is estimated that Cempoala had at least 80,000 people, with another 170,000 living in smaller, rural communities. Hernan Cortez and his men marched into this city in 1519, the first part of the Aztec empire that they had contacted. The governor of Cempoala was very hospitable in spite of threats from his Aztec overlords. The Spaniards' arrest of a group of Aztec tax collectors terrified the Totonac rulers but ultimately committed them to a rebellion against the empire. This was the first step in Cortez's ultimately successful strategy of raising revolts against the Aztecs by their subject peoples.

The Aztecs and Their Empire

Nearly all Mesoamericans had histories that began in mythical periods, at the creation of the world(s), or that had been gloriously embellished with heroic deeds and personalities. The Aztecs are no exception to this tradition of rewritten history. They are variously said to have come into the Valley of Mexico with Toltec refugees after the fall of Tula or from a mythical origin town called Aztlan, and it has been suggested that they were simply a pariah group that had been there all along. Late in the fourteenth century, several groups of an ethnic group who called themselves Mexica resided in at least three different cities of the basin. Apparently they were of very lowly social status but managed to make a name for themselves as fierce warriors. Accomplishing a number of notable military feats, they asked their principal patron, the ruler of the city of Azcapotzalco, for a piece of land where they could live together. They were given a set of rocky islets in a swampy and unpleasant zone. It was there that the Aztec, in accord with a prophecy, saw an eagle landing in a nopal cactus with a snake in his mouth and there that they founded their twin cities of Tenochtitlan and Tlatelolco (see Map 3.2).

Documentary and archaeological evidence indicates that the Aztec capital of Tenochtitlan was founded around A.D. 1325, with the earliest excavated construction of the Great Temple dating to about A.D. 1390 (Matos 1988:70). By this time there were about fifty city-states in the basin, all long established and many of them powerful. Most were located near, on the edge of, or even within the group of lakes that covered the floor of the valley. Many exploited the lake environment in a variety of ways, including wetland gardens called *chinampas*. Careful surveys indicate that these raised and drained fields eventually covered about 10,000 ha (25,000 acres) in and around the southernmost lake, Chalco, and supported about 180,000 people (Armillas 1971; Sanders 1970:9). Another 120,000 were sustained by the same means in the Texcoco region on the west side of the basin. The system consisted of draining the wetland margins by canals and filling the shallow lake edges with built-up stacks of waterplants and soil. The effect was a vast network of canals that had the multiple functions of drainage, sources of fresh soil for the fields, and routes of canoe transport.

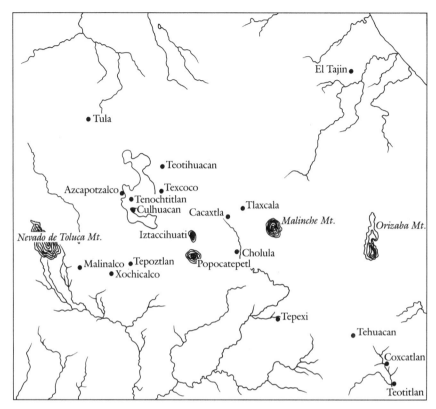

MAP 3.2   The Aztec empire

Farming families lived on their *chinampas* and grew multiple crops year-round. The *chinampa* system also acted as a method of land reclamation in somewhat the same way as the use of polders for drainage and freshwater rinsing of former seabeds in the Netherlands. The cities of Tenochtitlan and Tlatelolco enlarged their zones by this means. Standard irrigation systems and various forms of open field farming were in use as well.

Large numbers of migratory wildfowl were taken from the marshes, and large salamanders and even an algae *(spirulina)* were used for food. The Mexica also built timber cribs in the water and filled them with rubble and soil. However, these ingenious measures were not nearly enough to support much more than three-fourths of the dense populations of the valley, which totaled about 1.5 million in 1519. Tribute from outside the valley was necessary and the Aztecs suffered at first from lack of outside resources. Before solving the problems of food and urban layout, however, the Mexica had first to achieve political independence.

In 1428, a series of political and military crises developed in the relationships between the Mexica and their patrons, the Tepanec of Azcapotzalco. The current Tepanec ruler and his son were ambitious and seemed to be on their way to domination of the entire Basin of Mexico. This would have been the first step toward the building of a new empire. However, the ruler saw that the Mexica had become a threat to Tepanec hegemony and determined to destroy them. Political assassination, intrigue, and open warfare followed, with a series of battles won by the Mexica and their allies, two cities also in revolt against Azcapotzalco. By 1431, the Triple Alliance had triumphed and themselves dominated the basin and were on the threshold of going beyond it. The Aztecs, the united peoples of the valley, were led by Itzcoatl, the Mexica ruler; his chief councilor, Tlacaelel; and the great ruler of the city and state of Texcoco, Nezahualcoyotl. At this point, the personality of an outstanding individual can be seen against the more abstract background of evolutionary change.

The Mexica asked for engineering aid and labor from Texcoco, a long-established and cultured city, and received it. A great dike-causeway was constructed to barricade the western edge of the lake against the recurring and devastating floods of saltwater that ruined the *chinampas*. This effectively protected the Mexica capital as well. In 1431, freed from the threat of an overwhelming military force, the Mexica rebuilt their principal temple and apparently reorganized their capital city. Three major causeways connected the city with the mainland, but the best way of getting about was by canoe. Tens of thousands of canoes plied the waters of the lakes, bringing the produce of the southern *chinampas* to market and providing an unequaled means of economic integration. The Great Temple now became the structure whose ever-increasing bulk and spectacular form dominated the urban skyline for the next ninety years.

This set of buildings was recently excavated, and we gained extraordinarily revealing information (Matos 1988). All Mesoamerican communities appear to have been laid out in accordance with cosmological principles, even if only as simply as orientation along the cardinal directions. Most cities were more complexly designed than that, however, and the Great Temple in Tenochtitlan became the orienting point for the whole city (Aveni, Calnek, and Hartung 1988). A terraced platform supported two temples, dedicated respectively to Tlaloc, the god of rain, and to the patron tribal deity, Huitzilopochtli. Apparently at the equinox the sun rose in the notch between the temples; Tlaloc's temple was also aligned with a distant but visible mountain sacred to the rain god. The city's major streets were laid every 660 m (721 yards) from a spot in front of the temple, and other streets occurred every 220 m (241 yards). In the end, the Great Temple is best known as the location on which thousands of human victims were sacrificed.

Human sacrifice is the most notorious feature of Aztec culture. However, they did not invent the practice but were following and expanding a widespread religious custom probably already present in Olmec times. People to be used as sacrifices were gathered mainly through capture in war or as tribute from conquered territories. Some were persons of low status, slaves and servants offered by people of high rank. A few, however, were even of foreign noble status. Tlacaelel, the warrior-adviser to most Aztec emperors, is thought to have been responsible for the dramatic expansion of this kind of offering after the Aztecs came to power. It has been argued that one of his motivations was to inspire terror among conquered peoples or potential targets for imperial expansion. Another reason was in order to eliminate political enemies and suppress social dissent. However, the rationale was presented as a religious imperative that was largely a reformulated version of the Toltec concept of "sacred war." In this concept, human blood and hearts sustained the sun in its daily struggles with the powers of darkness. War therefore became a divinely sanctioned endeavor and the Aztecs a kind of hallowed people. A further incentive was added in that commoners could enhance their social status by the number of captives delivered for sacrifice.

Aztec social structure was based on the familiar aristocratic principle of leadership, with lower classes grouped into combined taxpayer and kinship units. These units were known as *calpulli*, or big house, and at least some of them were made up of patrilineal clans. In other cases, conveniently sized groups of taxpayers were aggregated into these administrative units. The Aztecs imposed several major functions on the *calpulli*, and these guided nearly every aspect of a commoner's everyday life. Land was owned by the *calpulli*, with the leader and his council periodically redistributing it. The size allocated to each family was adjusted to their changing circumstances, and theoretically all families had some excellent land and some of lesser quality. The families owed tribute to the city-state ruler or a noble patron family. This tax was paid in the form of the produce or manufactures of the *calpulli* and by labor. All *calpulli* were required to maintain a young men's school that taught basic subjects of deportment, religion, and military skills as well as other matters. Some particularly talented commoners might attend state-sponsored schools, where they and young aristocrats were prepared for state service as administrators, judges, and other functionaries. Each *calpulli* had a patron deity for which it maintained a small temple with an attached house for a resident priest. Most *calpulli* members were cremated upon death and their ashes buried with those of their ancestors under the pavement in front of the temple. The Aztecs were almost constantly at war from 1428 onward, and their armies required a constant supply of new soldiers. Men of military age went to war grouped according to *calpulli,* and thus these units formed a sort of militia. Police appointed from the *calpulli* were largely responsible for law and order within the cities. Most Aztecs lived their lives within the context of the *calpulli* system and thus were provided for in terms of basic needs, social security, physical security, education, and in other aspects.

Nobles at the top of Aztec society were descendants of rulers or relatives of present rulers. They had a number of privileges, including freedom from taxation, the right to build a two-story house, and the right to privately own land. Aristocratic estates came equipped with permanently indentured labor to work the land—serfs, to be exact. As noted earlier, most aristocrats were in state service in one form or another: army officers, emissaries, tribute collectors, governors, judges, and many other officials. "The nation has a special official for every activity, small though it were. Everything was so well recorded that no detail was left out of the accounts. There even officials in charge of sweeping . . . And so the officials of the Republic were innumerable" (Durán 1964:183). The thirty-eight provinces were governed either by Mexica governors or by formerly independent rulers who acted as such. Garrisons were placed at strategic points to be called upon in times of revolt or other peril. Otherwise the Aztecs made no attempt to assimilate conquered peoples.

State-sponsored long-distance merchants *(pochteca)* were esteemed but were also regarded as dangerous because of the menace to inherited social status created by private wealth. Thus, merchants were chastened by having to assume very humble clothing upon nearing Tenochtitlan. Most came in at night and hid their wealth immediately. However, the state used them as intelligence agents and valued their appraisals of the strengths and weaknesses of prospective conquests. Very long distance contacts were maintained, and it is reported that the Inca rulers knew about the Spanish conquest of Mexico soon after it had occurred.

Social mobility was partly available to commoners who distinguished themselves in war, mainly by captures. The more victims a soldier provided for the temples (and there were many besides the Great Temple), the more splendid his attire and the greater the privileges granted him and his family. The most successful warriors were granted temporary noble status together with small estates and the serf labor to work them. Upon their deaths, the family became commoners again, and the estate reverted to the ruler for redistribution. Present-day British life peerages are probably the closest social institution, although titles in the United Kingdom are emphatically not tied to human sacrifice.

Slavery was regarded as a temporary condition and was sometimes resorted to by a couple desperate to save their children in a famine. Children sold into slavery might be recovered later when conditions improved, if the parents could buy them out. Some slaves were criminals sentenced to provide restitution to their victim's family by means of their labor. This was a relatively small group of people in Aztec society, and one could not be born a slave. Unsuccessful gamblers sometimes ended up as slaves, with the ultimate wager presumably being one's freedom.

The empire expanded at a great rate and eventually reached into the western zones, eastward to the Gulf Coast, and down the Pacific coast of Guatemala. The Totonacs mentioned earlier had been early conquests outside the central plateau, and the next logical strategic step was to control the Isthmus of Tehuantepec as a means of gaining access to the famous cacao fields of Soconusco (Pacific coastal Guatemala). The Mixtec-Zapotec fortress of Guiengola was located at the edge of the isthmus, and the menace of this military power was probably the reason for the Aztec siege. The Aztecs failed in the siege but gained their objective of free passage by means of the marriage of a royal daughter to the Zapotec ruler.

The religious conceptions of the Aztecs were inherited from the past and, aside from the emphasis on human sacrifice, were unexceptional. Entire books have been written on Aztec religion, and only a sketchy account can be given here. The three major themes that pervaded Aztec theology were celestial creativity; rain, moisture, and agricultural fertility; and finally the state-fostered blood nourishment of the sun and earth by war and sacrifice. Multiple deities of both sexes made up a very crowded and active pantheon. The basic concept of "sacred war" has been mentioned and was essentially the same as that of the Toltecs. This view of the world as being continually on the verge of catastrophe was one that fit in with the idea of the four suns, or worlds, that had preceded the present universe. The present era was the Fifth Sun and would come to a cataclysmic end as had the others. The sun was aided in its fight to delay the end of the world by the continual offerings of human hearts and blood. The end of the world would eventually come on the end of a fifty-two-year cycle. The world had begun with a divine pair who had then become somewhat inert and withdrawn from intervention in human matters. However, this theme spurred the great philosopher-king, Nezahualcoyotl, to write some of his best poetry. The fertility theme was expressed largely by water gods and goddesses, plant deities, and—most appealing to many of us today— the hedonistic Xochipilli-Maquilxochitl, god of games and pleasure. Tlaloc, of course, was the most important of this group of supernaturals and had a number of assistants.

The Spanish landed on the mainland in 1517 and 1518, but came off badly in battles with the Maya, and it was not until Cortez organized his expedition in 1519 that a firm beachhead was established. Even then, the sponsoring governor of Cuba was hesitant about going inland and sent a punitive force to restrain Cortez and take control from him. This bureaucratic intervention was too late to be effective, however, because Cortez had already marched to Tenochtitlan and established himself at the court of Motecuhzoma II as the representative of the king of Spain. In a remarkable forced march, Cortez returned to the coast, defeated the Spanish leaders sent to supersede him, and recruited the rest of the newcomers for his army. He returned to Tenochtitlan to find the city in arms against his colleagues who had remained. They had committed a massacre and were besieged near the Great Temple. Some had been taken and sacrificed on the summit. Thereafter the events of the conquest were dramatic and varied but always led toward the ultimate downfall of the Aztec empire. An obvious advantage of the Spaniards was that of superior weapons and tactics. However, two other major factors were involved. Cortez accurately read the discontent within the empire due to heavy tribute payments and human sacrifice. He exploited these resentments to effectively raise a revolt against the Aztecs, and thousands of Indian allies accompanied him during the next two years of conquest. The second fatal element was that of the introduction of European diseases, against which neither the Aztecs nor any other Mesoamericans had immunities. Tens of thousands and, ultimately, millions died. It is estimated that 90 to 95 percent of the native population perished from diseases, overwork, famine, war, and other associated causes in the next 160 years. The population of the Valley of Mexico was reduced from 1.5 million to 70,000 in that time, and some areas were completely depopulated. The remnants of the elite were impoverished and degraded at the same time, and the old cultures died out rapidly under both this loss of leadership and that of conversion to Catholicism. Native cultural elements survived in part, in secret, and in attenuated forms. In the highlands of Guatemala, Indian children are still brought to a shaman soon after birth in order that their futures may be ascertained by use of the old 260-day calendar. In the Chiapas highlands, the Tzotzil Maya believe in thirteen-part souls as well as animal spirit companions. The *calpulli* as a form of social organization still exists in skeletal form in Tlaxcala, northeast of Mexico City and only a two-hour drive on the superhighway. It is still possible to see such remnants of the past and the ruins themselves, which are part of the cultural heritage of the modern nation-states of Guatemala, Mexico, Belize, Salvador, and Honduras. More broadly, these cultures are part of humanity's general heritage, and we are enriched by knowing about them.

4

The Central Andes
of South America:
Origins and Early Civilizations

Geography

Of all the world's locations for early civilizations, the Central Andean area is perhaps the most dramatic and exaggerated. An immense and broken geography of about 926,000 km² (357,000 mi²) was eventually occupied by complex cultures. Mountains rise to more than 5,400 m (18,000 feet) above sea level. Highland valleys of mainly north-south trend lend themselves to human occupation, given enough investment of time and labor. Plant and animal communities vary according to altitude, with zones of human occupation up to ca. 4,265 m (about 14,000 feet). Huge staircase terrace systems were built that even today awe the traveler. Indeed, the name of the mountain chain may derive from the first Spanish explorers, who were impressed by the *andenes* or terraces (Moseley 1992:29). Deserts of an Egyptian intensity are distributed along the Pacific coast, interrupted by fifty-five greater and lesser rivers that flow to the sea from the Andean chain. These rivers form oases that were cultivated and irrigated in ancient times. The deserts become more extreme as one proceeds from north to south until the Atacama Desert is reached, one of the driest areas of the world.

The offshore waters are just as remarkable. The Humboldt Current, created by onshore winds, is a north-flowing, cold-water upwelling that encourages the growth of a marine food chain of immense productivity. Millions of seabirds as well as huge numbers of fish, sea mammals, crustaceans, and other forms of life are attracted to and nurtured by this great oceanic feeding ground. In the normal cycles of the year, animals, plants, fish, and birds all feed well and flourish. However, from time to time the well-known El Niño reversal takes place, resulting in displacement of cold waters by warm currents closer to shore and catastrophic rainfall inland. Anchovies, a valuable food source for humans, birds, and larger fish alike, may decline as much as 87 percent in such years (Burger 1992:15). The desert landscape is subject to rapid erosion caused by flash floods and by the lack of stabilizing vegetation outside of cultivated areas. Therefore, drastic and rapid modification can take place, including the washing out of irrigation systems. The latter are also at risk from tectonic movements and general uplift along the coasts that may reverse water flow or displace the lengthy channels built for long-distance water transport.

On the eastern slope of the mountain masses, rivers flow into the Amazonian system with steep transitions between uplands and tropical lowlands. The highlanders expanded their activities into these lower zones to exploit the different plants, animals, and soils. Even with these extraordinary ecological contrasts and natural perils, the peoples of this area managed to create a series of magnificent civilizations that were well adapted to both landscape and climate.

Earliest Inhabitants and Cultures

If our assessments of the earliest entry into the New World are correct in both time and space, then sooner or later after the initial entry at 12,000 B.C. humans should have made their way through North and Central America and reached the southern continent (see Map 4.1). Somewhat surprisingly, this was a relatively rapid migration, although to the generations of people who were involved it must have seemed unending. Lynch (1983) thinks, along with earlier workers, that the altitudinal levels of the Andes encouraged north-south migration. By 11,000 B.C., early hunters camped by a stream and lived in wooden huts in central Chile (Dillehay 1989). By 8000 B.C., people had reached the tip of South America. These earliest inhabitants appear to have concentrated on hunting horses and solitary ground sloths, although they also killed or scavenged elephants. In many areas, camelids (especially llamas and guanacos) and deer were favored animals, and this was the case with the early (10000 to 5000 B.C.) culture of the Peruvian coast labeled the Paijin. In the Central Andes, people occupied Guitarrero Cave as early as 8600 B.C. From this

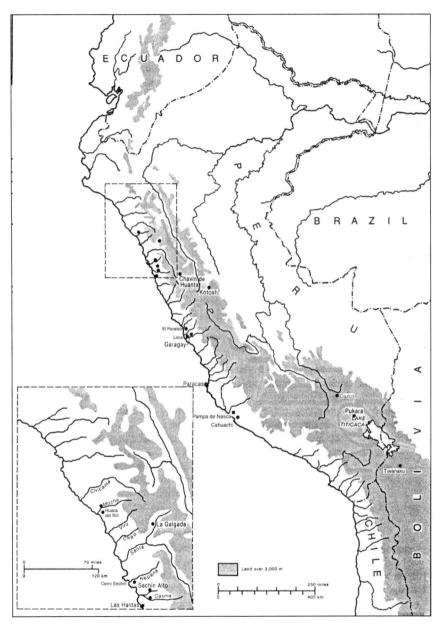

MAP 4.1   The Andes, showing Initial Period, Early Horizon, and Early
Intermediate Period sites

base, hunters went forth to obtain deer and several smaller animals, including skunk and opossum. A favorite game bird still extant in the area is the tinamou, a family of delectable quail- and chicken-sized creatures easily hunted. Seasonal migration was a way of life by that time and perhaps always had been. This meant yearly cycles of travel from one altitude range to another to exploit different animal communities. Very little is known about the plant-gathering activities that must have taken place, although the area is renowned for its many wild tubers, including the ancestral forms of the potato.

By 7500 B.C. there were several specialized lifeways in the Andean area, each attuned to the ecological peculiarities of its home zone. However, about that time, human cultures were also shifting to a more closely adapted form of life that emphasized residence for at least several months of the year in one zone. In this shift, because of animal extinctions, climatic change, and other factors, human groups were intensively exploring the possibilities of plant food production and, in fact, had already begun such production. People living in Guitarrero Cave at about 8500 B.C. were using large amounts of beans, which is evidence of domestication. There are also indications that they were eating hot peppers and lima beans as well. To these carbohydrate-rich plants were added several tubers over the next centuries of occupation. Lynch comments that the shift was probably gradual and evolutionary rather than revolutionary (1983:125). Additions of newly adapted plants to regional inventories followed over the long period needed for the process of transferral from one altitude to another. Maize (corn), probably from Central America, appeared perhaps as late as 2000 B.C. but possibly as early as 5500 B.C. Instead of becoming a major food staple, in the Andes it was largely used as a carbohydrate supplement and for making an intoxicating beverage *(chicha)*.

The domestication of large camelid animals distinguishes South America from Mesoamerica in this period of food production development. Llamas and perhaps alpacas were being corralled and herded by 4200 B.C. in some of the high *puna* (savanna) around Junín, Peru. However, another of the many mysteries surrounding this transition from hunting and gathering to agriculture is the domestication of the guinea pig, that ubiquitous item of the present-day and prehistoric Andean diet. The results of these incompletely known (and no doubt tortuous) processes were full-blown food complexes that eventually sustained villages, towns, and cities and the millions of people in them. It is noteworthy that the sequences of domestications appear to have begun (ca. 8500 B.C.) and to have achieved sufficiency (ca. 1800 B.C.) at the same times as those in Mesoamerica. There were significant differences, however. One was the presence of large numbers of meat animals, small as they may have been in the case of the guinea pig. Second, the presence of beasts of burden that could operate at high altitudes was a relief to humans, who therefore did not have to pack quite as much themselves. Third, the food plant inventory of the Andes is quite different and heavily dependent on tuberous plants rather than on grains as in Mesoamerica.

These aggregations of plants and animals were regionalized and segregated by altitude. One problem for all of the later complex cultures was to vertically integrate enough regions to insure reasonable variety and security in food supplies. First, however, small communities of people who were finding their way into food production also had to work out the basic organizational problems of living in villages. Further, they also faced the difficulties of dealing with neighboring communities and of dealing with necessary tasks beyond their own capacities. For the latter—building extensive irrigation works, for example—they needed the help and cooperation of their neighbors. We now turn to the establishment of those basic village communities and to the development of the networks of trade, religious practices, labor cooperatives, and other social mechanisms that made complex life possible and ever changing.

Early Villages and Regional Centers (5500–2000 B.C.)

Some of the earliest and perhaps *the* earliest villages in the area appeared on the desert coast. Moseley has argued that these communities were based largely on the resources of the sea, which he called "the maritime foundations of Peruvian civilization" (1975). An immensely rich and productive harvest lay immediately offshore for those human groups who could develop the technology and techniques needed to exploit it. As noted earlier, the Humboldt Current is an upwelling of cold water that supports a varied and incredibly lavish food chain, much of which can be converted into human food. Fishing, netting birds, hunting sea mammals, and gathering shell fish, crustaceans, and other forms of seafood were apparently done by several groups along the coast by 5500 B.C. and perhaps as early as 6500 B.C. at the site of Paloma on the Central Coast of what is now Peru. Demonstrating the importance of the maritime economic base, the most complex of these early cultures eventually appeared along the 600-km (375-mile) coast off which lay what are known as fishery hot spots. These maritime maxima today yield about 1,000 tons per km^2 (2.3 short tons per mi^2) of sea per year. About forty sites are known along this coast from this sedentary preceramic and preagricultural period.

Paloma was a large village of fishing families who lived in round houses built of reed bundles tied to a light wooden framework, occasionally supplemented by whale ribs. These domed-shaped houses also became burial places for family members as in the case of the famous Hut 12 at the nearby site of Chilca (Donnan 1964). Fishing nets, lines, weights, and other maritime paraphernalia were found. Analysis of the skulls of the men showed damage to the bony structures of the ears by continual diving in cold water at Paloma (Benfer 1990) and Huaca Prieta (Burger 1992:103). Some gardening was done at Paloma; cultivated plants included squash, beans, and gourds, the latter being used for net floats among other things. Paloma was also in contact with groups in the higher areas of the Andes and traded for obsidian and even for a monkey from distant jungles. Seashells exotic to the area also came through exchange. Human feces at Paloma were largely made up of bones from small fish such as anchovies and sardines, directly reflecting the diet. However, as Moseley (1992) points out, the fiber for nets and lines as well as wood for heating and cooking had to be obtained from the land, and after 3000 B.C. a great deal of cotton was raised along the coast as well as new food items.

Population increase pushed these economic developments, as is well documented at Paloma and other sites. Many inland villages, located in the strips of arable land along the rivers, became much more agricultural. It is probably not coincidental that the first large platforms appeared at about this time. There is little doubt that these and later communal structures were built for religious purposes. At El Aspero, on the shoreline of the central coast, there are seventeen large and small mounds and platforms. One of the largest, which dates to about 2800 B.C. (perhaps to 3000 B.C.), supported a building of several rooms. Evidence of burnt offerings and possible human sacrifices were found. In another building atop a neighboring platform were thirteen broken, unbaked clay figurines; eleven of them were female and of those four were pregnant. Moseley (1992) suggests that shamanistic curing practices may have been involved. Over the next thousand years this tradition of community religious centers became a more fixed and complex element in Andean life. The center of El Paraiso (Chuquitanta) is the largest of these preceramic centers, and construction on it began by 2000 B.C. It is located in the Chillon Valley and is perhaps the earliest of the centers to show a U-shaped layout of its buildings. Seven of the approximately fourteen mounds are arranged in this pattern; the open end of the U faces the mountains, not the sea. A reconstructed building is very complex, with about twenty-five rooms arranged around a central room. Fire pits were found in the floor of the central room. The buildings seem to have been residences for families of importance (Fung de Pineda 1988:72). Perhaps they were supported by many other families who owed them allegiance. Successful as El Paraiso was for many generations, it was abandoned abruptly after a couple of hundred years.

People of the Northern Highlands were constructing ceremonial and residential buildings nearly as early as the people on the coast. Small temple construction began at Huaricoto and La Galgada by 2800 B.C. and perhaps earlier. Kotosh is a very early site, with construction possibly dating to 2400 B.C. There were at least six highland centers by 2200 B.C. These sites appear to have functioned as religious centers, as shown by llama sacrifices as well as burnt offerings. One early building at Kotosh has a wall with human arms and crossed hands modeled in stucco below two niches. There are closed courtyard groups as well as U-shaped arrangements that appear to be later.

Meanwhile, most or all the people of these communities may have lived in relatively humble housing, such as the square, earth-lodge–type dwellings at Huaca Prieta or the more fragile and perishable reed huts of Asia. Burger mentions the "notable lack of lavish burials at any Late Preceramic sites" (1992:36) and concludes that these highland and lowland temple centers represent "small, unstratified theocratic polities" (1992:42). At first glance, the construction projects carried out between 3000 and 2500 B.C. appear to be beyond the capacities of village-level societies in their requirements for sustained planning and building coordination. However, Burger and others make a convincing case for the power of religious motivation in creating labor cooperatives. Although there were leaders, they appear to have been weak and decentralized. The preceramic burials at La Galgada reflect this lack of social distinctions. The dead were entombed either in sealed-up temple chambers or in gallery tombs within the temple. Burial chambers were repeatedly reopened for the interment of newly dead persons. Men, women, and children were all placed in the tombs, and the items placed with the dead are about the same for people of the same sex and age group.

Early relationships between highlands and lowlands show the development of the first forms of the feature of vertical integration discussed earlier. Cotton and gourds are natives of the humid tropical eastern slopes and foothills of the Andes, not the desert coasts. These items might have been exchanged for the iodine-rich ocean salt and fish needed to combat endemic goiter and cretinism in the highlands (Burger 1992:32) and may have been the basis of the much more diverse later trade between the zones. However, ancestral forms of cotton and gourds also may have been obtained from the moister Ecuadorean and Colombian coasts to the north.

Growth and Transformations (2000–800 B.C.)

From ca. 2000 to 800 B.C., Central Andean societies developed many of the patterns that can be seen in later Inca culture and those of their predecessors. Economic, social, and religious transformations were apparently accompanied by militarism. Technological change also occurred, with ceramics being introduced ca. 2000 B.C. from coastal cultures of Ecuador and Colombia where pottery was invented by 3200 B.C. The earliest ceramics are bottle gourd in shape and reflect the earlier use of actual gourds as containers. Textile production, the other supreme Andean craft, also developed early, as shown by the ancient cloth from Huaca Prieta on the North Coast.

U-shaped centers became the dominant site layout after 1800 B.C. They occur in the highlands and lowlands of the north, and the pattern lasted for about one thousand years. On the desert coast, the Casma Valley centers of Sechin Alto and Las Aldas are among the largest known of these sites. In Sechin Alto there is a gigantic, stone-faced platform, nearly 3 million cubic meters (nearly 4 million cubic yards) in mass, built before 1650 B.C. (Fung de Pineda 1988:88), with wings of lower buildings in front of it forming the arms of the U. Sunken courts are also features of many of these early centers.

Moseley has suggested that the platforms were stages for display of public ritual, whereas the sunken courts might represent the interior of the earth from which the first people ascended, according to later Inca myth (1992:110–112). The U-shaped buildings may represent an orientation toward the rising sun and the mountains, at least in the case of the coastal centers (Moseley 1992:121). Religion became an early and strong motivating force in Andean cultural evolution. Burger comments that later traditional Peruvian communities held rights to land through a founding ancestor or a supernatural (a divine animal, bird, fish, and so on) and that individuals participated in these rights only as members of the social group. Religious activity by the individual validated his or her right to group membership and therefore access to economic security (Burger 1992:37). Some notion of the religious ideology of the time comes from polychrome friezes found in a building of a late U-shaped complex at Garagay. Fanged supernatural creatures with spider features are shown, and Burger links these creatures to divination ritual and irrigation water control, based on analogies to much later Andean religious patterns (1992:63).

Through the centuries, literally hundreds of small and large centers were built in the various valleys of the coast and highlands. There is no indication of these being elite class tomb buildings as in later times, but there is little doubt that the religious leaders were accumulating political power that they would use to transform themselves into a hereditary elite—in a word, aristocrats. But, for this period, it appears that each of the centers was built by a relatively small society, each of which controlled a small irrigation system. These groups may have been analogous to the later Peruvian *ayllu*, a variety of clan based on kinship traced though both the male and female lines (Moseley 1992:49). Such groups probably had relatively diffuse authority. However, even such leadership, given its ability to religiously motivate masses of people, was capable of completing the great numbers of construction projects carried out during the period.

A group of North Coast valleys centered on the Chicama was the location of a culture that appeared about 1500, the Cupisnique. Related but politically jumbled groups built a diversity of structures at several places, resulting in somewhat disordered centers. Caballo Muerto has eight mound complexes, and there are fifteen at Purulén. Many of the buildings were decorated with modeled adobe sculptures that emphasize jaguar and spider motifs. Both creatures are associated with plant life, thus showing a beneficent mode, but they are also shown with human trophy heads, thereby displaying their predatory aspects. Jaguars are still regarded as the alter egos for shamans and priests today in tropical South America, and this is probably the best interpretation of the meaning of the feline motif.

We can also see signs of the violence apparently inherent in human cultures, with evidence of raids in the form of human trophy heads at the preceramic village of Asia (Moseley 1992:107–108) and at Salinas de Santa, where piles of sling stones were found on two sides of a village (Topic and Topic 1987:50). About 1400 B.C., a military monument was built at Cerro Sechin in the Casma Valley in which sculptures of human heads and other body parts were placed around a large building. The depictions of "trophies" are mixed with carvings of giant warrior figures armed with clubs. Formal fortifications, and therefore formal warfare, apparently came later.

About 1400 B.C. people on the coast abandoned the older floodplain irrigation and developed newer and more extensive systems of canals. These new operations were based on taking out water from the necks of rivers that came down from the highlands at the points where the rivers broke out of their canyons and gorges and flowed into flatter country. With these arrangements, it was possible to irrigate larger areas of the alluvial fans in the lower valleys. This sort of system was probably required because of population growth and the consequent need for more food. However, the more complex irrigation complexes also created their own imperatives, in that more people and more organization were needed to create and maintain them. The shift in the economic basis also created food production systems worth fighting about.

In the Southern Highlands, around and near the great Lake Titicaca (3,810 m [12,500 feet] above sea level), herding and farming villages had appeared as early as 1400 B.C. A gradual growth of population led to the development of combined pastoral and agricultural systems around Chiripa. The people grew high-altitude grain, quinoa, and potatoes and herded the camelid llamas and alpacas. About 1000 B.C. people from these villages built a large platform with a sunken court at the top surrounded by small rectangular buildings. Most artistic expression was in the form of elaborate and cleverly decorated pottery, including some ceramic trumpets. Erickson (1993) has studied the extensive raised field areas in this area north of the lake and concluded that the technique was begun ca. 1000 B.C. He also argues convincingly that the system of raised fields is the aggregate result of individual family and kin group effort and not of massive, centralized state organization.

We have spoken here of art as mainly in the service of aesthetic requirements of kinship and religious groups. Separately, formal artistic expression developed early, in the preceramic cultures, and ca. 2000 B.C. people at the village of Huaca Prieta on the central coast began to decorate gourds and textiles with images of doubled-headed creature and winged condors. Buildings decorated with modeled adobe were constructed inland about 1800 B.C. at Moxeke and at the Sechin sites by 1721 B.C. These structures were clearly religious in function, and huge, fanged feline heads were among the motifs. After 1500 B.C. trophy heads were commonly used at other temple centers elsewhere in the Andes and along the coast. Metallurgy, in the form of beaten thin sheets of gold, was used as early as 1700 B.C. (Burger 1992:127). Somewhat later, ca. 1000 B.C., villages in the Southern Highlands began to work copper, tin, and bronze. This activity was the beginning of the great Andean tradition of metalworking that led to such exquisite works of craftsmanship that they were proclaimed as great art both by the Spanish conquerors and modern viewers.

In this period, transformation of the economic base, religion, and social structure went along with a gradual increase in scale. The later monuments (ca. 800 B.C.) of the Moche Valley are much larger; they are associated with larger irrigation systems and imply larger political systems. Indeed, the Pozorskis suggest that small states may have developed in the Casma Valley during this time (Pozorski and Pozorski 1987:20–21; S. Pozorski 1988:116–117). However, about 800 B.C., regional developments in the Casma and elsewhere were truncated when they were replaced by a new and different culture.

The Early Horizon (Chavin)

The Chavin expansion is the first of three large-scale religious and military events in Andean prehistory by which one region imposed its cultural patterns on other regions. The first of these unifying processes, also known as the Chavin Horizon, is also one of the most interesting because it pioneered some of the techniques that were used by the later Inca.

Chavin de Huantar is a regional temple center in the Central Highlands, founded about 900 B.C., which was long before the Chavin cult was more than a localized matter. The principal building is the Old Temple, which is a U-shaped structure with the open end of the U oriented toward the rising sun. The temple appears to be made of solid rock. However, this massive building actually is mostly stone and dirt fill faced with cut stone. It is also far from solid, inasmuch as 25 percent of its volume is made up of channels, ventilators, and labyrinthine passageways. At least eight gallery systems are known, and undoubtedly there are many more in unexplored parts of the structure. Hidden within a gallery in the heart of the building is a giant sculpture (the Lanzón) that is an image of a partly human and partly feline creature. This was the main god of the center and perhaps was also an oracle. Hundreds of air ducts keep the interior cool. Water running through the drains, as shown by a modern trial, creates an amplified and impressive rushing sound. Inside the arms of the U was a sunken circular court around which are sculptures of crouching jaguars and marching supernatural creatures (Burger 1992:130–144). Altogether, these and other features of the temple were carefully calculated to impress. Further, oracles, secreted idols, galleries, and hidden patios were features of much later Andean temples. This demonstrates the deep continuities in Andean religious practices.

The jaguar god was not the only deity worshipped at Chavin, however. Many ornamental and a few free-standing sculptures were in, on, and around the temple. These show partly human, partly feline figures, sometimes ornamented with snakes. The Staff Deity is a feline god who holds staffs that are double-headed serpents. The cayman (a crocodile) and the huge harpy eagle were also important. Both are fearsome predators of the tropical lowlands east of the Andes but not of the mountains. Some of the most intimidating aspects of nature were symbolized by these earthly and supernatural figures. It is also clear that the world, as visualized by the people at Chavin, was not limited to the mountainous areas. All three principal gods—jaguar, crocodile, and snake—as well as the harpy eagle are natives of the tropical forests. The most likely explanation of this is that the origin myths for humanity and its food plants were derived from the tropical forest cultures and therefore the animals active in such myths were also adopted.

The tropical forest is not the sole source for Chavin religious ideas. As Burger makes clear, the site has many coastal architectural features. The religion that Chavin represents, then, was a fusion of ideas from at least three zones of the area: highlands, tropical forest, and the desert coasts. The symbolism of Chavin art implies a religion that emphasized the maintenance of harmony and balance, as between male and female, or other natural opposites (Burger 1992:180). The original temple at Chavin was greatly enlarged between 500 and 200 B.C. The resultant New Temple reflects these principles of opposition and resolution. It had twin shrines on top of the platform, although its platform also had galleries and other interior features.

Population around the center grew from the original 500 to 1,000 at 400 B.C. and then to about 2,500 by 200 B.C. Many social differences had developed by that time. A permanent elite had appeared, probably as the result of increased trade and temple tribute from merchants. Part- and full-time craft specialists were at work around Chavin as well. Differences in status were reflected in housing and diet. The elite lived in stone houses and dined on young tender llamas, whereas the majority of people lived in adobe houses and ate tough old animals.

Increased trade and the growing wealth of the Chavin temple center were due to the vastly increased use of domesticated llamas as pack animals after 500 B.C. Burger points out that llamas carry 20 to 60 kg (44 to 132 lbs.) for 15 to 20 km (9 to 12 miles) per day and that one driver can handle between ten and thirty animals. The beasts eat from the roadside and sustain themselves. This is a huge improvement over the relatively small amounts of weight that humans can carry, especially at high altitudes, and avoids the problems of carrying large quantities of food. Even commodities such as potatoes and grains could be moved economically (Burger 1992:210). With large numbers of animals and pack trains, it also became advantageous to build roads, and the first large-scale road building began on the North Coast during this time (Beck 1979, as quoted in Hyslop 1984). Burger concludes that the Chavin cult was spread largely by the mechanism of widespread trade and by the cultural means of a group of shared religious ideas (1992:213). However, it is also possible that warfare was involved. The Pozorskis conclude that the Casma Valley was probably conquered by invaders from the highlands (Pozorski and Pozorski 1987:118–125). The nearby Santa Valley has twenty-one hilltop citadels that date from this time, reflecting an insecure and violent environment.

Violently or peaceably, about 500 B.C. the Chavin cult probably began to spread on the basis of a religion that offered something to everyone. Its way was made easier by the prior collapses of the old temple centers between 900 and 700 B.C. These failures were often abrupt. Las Aldas, for example, was abandoned while a new staircase was being finished, and later squatters lived on top of the formerly sacred buildings and dumped trash over them. In the case of the North Coast, there is some evidence of massive flooding from an El Niño and consequent ecological deterioration afterwards. New communities that were established were of a radically different nature. San Diego, in the Casma Valley, was a town-sized community but without any large mounds. In addition, maize (corn) was introduced massively and suddenly into the Casma (Pozorski and Pozorski 1987:119, 124). The natural disasters may have discredited the local shrines and *huacas* upon which the local farmers had depended to avert such catastrophes. A reformed religion might have been very attractive under such circumstances.

There were cultures that show very little Chavin contact and influence. On the South Coast, the Paracas peninsula is a projection of the desert into the Pacific. By 450 B.C. the fishing villages located here had developed a burial cult that was very distinctive. The villagers wrapped the bodies of the dead, without social distinction, in yards of cloth and buried them in bottle-shaped family tombs dug into the soft marl. After about a hundred years new mortuary customs appeared; then the bodies were wrapped into bundles and placed in subterranean rooms. At about this same time social distinctions appeared in the form of more elaborate textiles for a few burials. Some of these burials have textiles with feline motifs and a tenuous linkage with Chavin art. The elaborate textiles were woven on backstrap looms, and Paul estimates that the cloth in a high-status burial represented about 46,000 hours of labor (more than ten years) by a number of women (Paul 1990:33). Most of the elaborate textiles were decorated by embroidery and many are of alpaca wool imported from the Southern Highlands. Large amounts of cotton were probably grown regionally for use in fabrics. Brightly decorated textiles show masked human figures, various birds, and felines as well as geometric motifs. Paracas weavings are excellently executed and admired as works of art today. They once served as status symbols for males who led the kinship units that made up the basic structure of society in this region. Turbans, tunics, shawls, and other items of clothing are represented. The bundles also contain food, ornaments, weapons, small dried-up animals, and an amazingly vibrant style of polychrome pottery. Textile motifs symbolized clans and families, and the mummy bundles wrapped in such embroidered cloths therefore functioned as ancestral figures for these kinship units.

By 200 B.C. the Chavin cult lost its panregional appeal, militarism was definitely on the upswing in highlands and lowlands, and the new permanent elites were often at each other's throats. The old self-organized Chavin cult gave way to more regionalized cultures that flowered into fully developed civilizations.

Early Civilizations: Moche, Nazca, the Central Coast, and Tiwanaku (200 B.C.–A.D. 600)

In the strictest sense of the definition given in Chapter 1, the Initial Period and Early Horizon (Chavin) cultures were not full-blown civilizations. Instead, they were transitional complex cultures that led to completely reformulated institutions along hierarchical lines. In this sense they were like the precocious Neolithic centers of the Near East: Jericho and Chatal Huyuk. The cultures of the Central Andes from 200 B.C. to A.D. 600 do fall into the category of civilized societies. A number of Central Andean cultures made this transition successfully, but I will discuss only three of them—enough to give an idea of their flavor and variety. Two of the examples are coastal: the Moche on the North Coast and the Nazca in the south. The third is the remarkable civilization of the Southern Highlands, Tiwanaku.

The Moche

By 200 B.C. on the North Coast, several valleys had been divided into segments by small principalities. In the Viru Valley, two forts and four defensible communities were founded. These communities and their leaders were in conflict with one another. Within the next two centuries, one of these groups prevailed and established a capital that dominated a population of at least fifty thousand who lived on the basis of extensive irrigated lands. New fortifications were built to protect the irrigation network against outsiders. To the north, the Moche Valley had been politically unified by about the same time (A.D. 1), and its capital had been established at the city of the same name. Within the next two hundred years, Moche established its dominance over most of the North Coast and conquered valleys such as Viru to its south. By A.D. 250, construction of two gigantic platform complexes had begun, the Huaca del Sol (the sacred place of the sun) and the Huaca de la Luna (the sacred place of the moon). Eventually, as the Moche empire enlarged, the *huacas* became huge, with courtyards, staircases, buildings, temples, burials, mausoleums, and other features. The sun platform became the residence for rulers, whereas the moon platform may have been the principal place of worship (Conklin and Moseley 1988:149–150).

Politically, Moche was a military conquest state, with perhaps five administrative levels. Topic believes that the moon platform was the ruler's residence, with the principal nobles housed on the sun platform (T. L. Topic 1982:279–280). The state was ruled by divine kings who are depicted in beautifully modeled and painted ceramics as well as in murals. The next level was that of the noble administrators and then probably a series of bureaucrats who corresponded to the later *karaka* class. In Inca times, the *karakas* were the heads of *ayllu*. There were two of them for each clan, and they reported up the line to more powerful managers. Moseley sees a great deal of continuity in organizational principles between the early states and the much later Inca empire (1992:49–79). The Moche also incorporated formerly independent rulers into the system if they collaborated.

Topic has defined at least four social classes at Moche. Each had its distinctive housing and burial patterns (1982:269–270). By A.D. 600, the city had spread over an area of about 1 km² (.38 mi²) and probably contained about fifteen thousand people. Each of the subordinate valleys had a *huaca* by this time that was the tangible expression of Moche political power and sacred authority. The state was linked by a system of relay runners who carried, of all things, lima beans with cryptic markings on them. As will be seen in the section on the Inca, a great deal of information can be transmitted by means of a rather compact and restricted code. State messengers operated along a network of roads that were a standard 10 m (33 feet) wide with shelters on platforms for the runners every few miles.

The lives of commoners were highly organized. They probably furnished taxes in the form of labor to the state for construction and other projects. The Huaca del Sol contains over 143 million bricks, even though only about one-third of it is left today. These bricks were laid up in distinct columns and are marked with over one hundred maker's symbols. Columns and marks probably indicate tax-paying units, possibly the lineages making up the *ayllu*. Most people lived in one-story adobe-walled houses with small walled courtyards. Many people practiced a craft, such as weaving or metallurgy, either part time or full time. Judging by the elegant jewelry found in rare, unlooted tombs, there were also highly skilled artisans, probably attached to noble households.

Most people were farmers, living in villages dispersed among the extensive irrigation canals. Huge irrigation systems were developed. A canal 120 km (75 miles) long is still in use today in the Chicama Valley. The people cultivated a great variety of plants, exploited many forms of sea life, hunted deer and other wild animals, and occasionally ate llamas as well. The latter were mainly used for their wool and for pack trains, however. There was considerable travel along the coast, and voyages were made to the Chincha Islands, where vast mounds of bird guano were mined for fertilizer. It is uncertain that the Moche had more than the small reed fishing boats that they had inherited from the ancient past, but it seems likely that bulk loads such as fertilizer would have been better shipped by sea in large craft.

The Moche are renowned for their arts. There are apparently a great many subjects, but Christopher Donnan has analyzed the materials and shown that fewer than twenty-five themes make up most of the scenes (Donnan 1976). Hand-to-hand combat is a common motif. Possibly the most important is the presentation theme. This is a fairly complex ritual in which several persons and men-jaguars dispose of captives. There is always a dominant figure (a warrior priest) who is seated on a throne. The captives are bled and their blood collected in goblets, which are offered to the warrior priest. The extraordinary tombs found in 1987 at Huaca Sipan in the Lambayeque Valley were of just such a notable person. Large amounts of gold and silver jewelry of fine workmanship were recovered. Many of the items (knives, goblets, and so on) in at least one tomb were of the special forms shown in presentation scenes. Although from our cultural perspective these are ghastly and even diabolical scenes, the rituals they represent were probably well within the current religious thought of the time. Additionally, it can be shown that elites of any period and culture are often characterized by ruthlessness and the use of intimidation. When also backed by ideological sanction, it is possible to justify nearly anything. The Moche did build a great and glorious civilization, but it was of the archaic kind in which the majority of the population supported a tiny group of privileged people at the top of society.

By whatever means were at hand, then, the Moche formed a large state made up of the most populated valleys of the North Coast. This state lasted until about A.D. 600, when a natural calamity fatally weakened it (Moseley 1992:183).

The Central Coast

Near the present-day city of Lima, and within sight of the sea, the great oracle center of Pachacamac was established on a *huaca* about A.D. 200. This grew to be an enormous complex of platforms, patios, walled areas, rooms, and passageways. It was the political and sacred center for the Lurín and Rimac Valleys and later a center for pilgrimages from all over the Andes. Very little is known of the culture history of Pachacamac in spite of early work and because of ruthless looting from colonial times to the present day. However, because it was one of the most sacred places in the Inca Empire, we have some eyewitness accounts of the operations of the *huaca* and its attendants. Another major city, dating to between A.D. 200 and 600, is apparently concealed by modern Lima (located in the Rimac).

The Nazca

Three hundred and twenty km (200 miles) south of the Rimac Valley on the Central Coast are the five most important valleys of the South Coast:

Chincha, Pisco, Ica, Grande (Nazca), and Acari. This zone is extraordinarily dry; in some places rainfall has *never* been recorded. However, the
runoff from the Andes creates rivers here just as on the North Coast.
These streams run underground for parts of their courses and then resur-
face, creating oases along the valley floors.

The Paracas peninsula, mentioned earlier, is located in this area, but its
heyday as an innovative area was done by 175 B.C. The inland valleys had
been developed into ingeniously cultivated patches and strips of ground.
Possibly by this time a system of tunnels carrying water from springs and
aquifers to fertile soils had been started. As Moseley points out, this irrigation method nearly duplicates one that is also very ancient in the Near
East, which in Iran is called the *qanat* system (Moseley 1992:186). This
technique compensated somewhat for the harsh dryness of the climate.
However, those conditions ultimately limited the expansion and elabora-
tion of civilization on the South Coast.

Nazca culture represents a more elemental version of the political development on the better-favored North Coast. In other respects it was a
rich and elaborate culture. A large center was built at Cahuachi perhaps as
early as 200 B.C., but it appears to have been nearly vacant of permanent
population. More than forty *huacas* or modified natural hills have been
found but no large-scale housing areas as at the Moche capital or other
Andean urban centers. A small permanent group of resident leaders probably lived on some of the platforms. The supporting population that used
the center lived most of their lives in their scattered home villages, coming
to Cahuachi only for ceremonial occasions. These occasions included
agricultural fertility rites. During these ceremonies, trophy heads were
taken, but from whom is unknown. The farmer participants played pan
pipes and engaged in large feasts. Burial of dead family members was another activity carried out at Cahuachi, and extensive (mostly looted)
cemeteries are located on the hillsides. The center was also a place full of
sacred geography that linked it to the famous markings and pictures in the
desert. Pilgrimages may well have taken place to Cahuachi to visit the
huacas as in other places and other times in the Andes (Silverman 1988).
It appears that the leadership of the Nazca region was diverse and that
there was more of a confederacy of clans and families than any centralized
political system. The forty or more *huacas* therefore were the hubs of political as well as sacred activities.

Nazca pottery and textiles are famous. By this time (A.D. 300) all of the
known weaving techniques were in use on the South Coast. Polychrome

pottery showed the various deities and mythical figures important to people of the region. These included "rayed" or "feline" figures, which may actually be otters that are to be found in irrigation ditches of the area today and were therefore associated with water and fertility (Sawyer 1961:287). The great figures and lines in the desert were created by clearing the pampas floors of stone, leaving the motifs. These symbols are animal, bird, and mythical figures, the same as those found on the ceramics. The straight lines were probably ritual walkways. Some of them were associated with water sources and therefore with agriculture, life, and fertility.

The Nazca was a spectacular, but short-lived, florescence in an unlikely area. It lasted until about A.D. 550, when a severe drought set in over the Andes and probably brought about a collapse of high culture on the South Coast.

Tiwanaku

Tiwanaku is a very large city that once existed half a day's walk from the southeastern shore of Lake Titicaca. Tiwanaku was reported by the sixteenth-century Spanish historian Cieza de Leon but had fallen into ruins by that time. The Incas regarded the lake and its islands as their ancestral homeland. The zone clearly had special importance for all Andean cultures.

Tiwanaku was probably founded by 200 B.C., but its great period of building and expansion did not begin until about A.D. 100. There is some indication that intensive agricultural works were started much earlier, but they were expanded on a large scale beginning about A.D. 100. According to Erickson's interpretation, the system was created not by state bureaucrats but by kinship units. With the appearance of state-level society, the system was expanded to create surpluses for the support of the administrators and other elite (Erickson 1993). In the Pampa Koani district, networks of canals, ridged fields, and raised fields eventually covered 100 km^2 (ca. 38 mi^2), and this was not the only agricultural zone. In this ingenious system, the surrounding ditches generate fog that forms around the plants and protects them from frost. Potatoes and other tubers grown in these and other fields supported about 365,000 people. The people also consumed llamas and food stuffs imported from lower altitudes. The rural population (about 250,000) lived dispersed in houses built on low mounds among the fields. Several large platform mounds connected by causeways supported the headquarters of the administrators who operated this complex system (Kolata 1986, 1991).

The city of Tiwanaku itself is dominated by two huge stone-faced platforms, each of which has a sunken court in its summit. High quality stone buildings stood atop the platforms, which were entered through a series of extraordinary gateways. Most of these entrances were made of single massive blocks of stone and some are carved. The most famous gate is the Gateway of the Sun; the main motif on it may be a late version of the old Chavin Staff God. A great deal of stone sculpture in a very distinctive style is to be found at Tiwanaku and sites with which it was in contact. A courtyard housed a large number of stelae that may include gods captured from conquered peoples subject to Tiwanaku. Sculptures in the forms of human heads and skulls that are tenoned into the walls decorated at least one building, showing that trophy heads were ritually important here as elsewhere. The great platforms with their impressive buildings were the residences and offices of the ruling elite, whereas the mass of the population lived in humble quarters.

The capital had as many as 40,000 people in it and another 75,000 lived in other urban centers. At least four towns or small cities were subordinate to the capital at Tiwanaku. Colonies were located in the South Coast, on the eastern side of the Andes, and far to the south in what is now northern Chile. Maize, coca, tropical birds, medicinal herbs, and other products were extracted from these zones. Herding had long been a primary activity in the highlands around Tiwanaku, and the llamas were used in pack trains to maintain contact with colonial or allied communities. Alpacas furnished high grade wool for textiles and clothing (Kolata 1991).

The elite classes at Tiwanaku spread their influence and power on the basis of alliances and colonization and perhaps by warfare. Its special ideology was spread throughout its area of influence and may have been a factor in the acceptance of political linkages. Most scholars regard Tiwanaku as an imperial system, incorporating into it many ethnic and linguistic groups and vertically integrating large areas of the Andes zone for the first time. It was one of the most persistent of all Andean cultures, lasting until about A.D. 1000. Its enormously productive cultivation zones, painfully developed in the swamplands, may have been drowned by a sudden and severe rise in the level of Lake Titicaca. At any rate, the hinterlands and the city were abandoned together and never reoccupied. Salt deposits in the former growing areas also hint at another problem. The buildup of saline deposits is often a problem in long-term irrigation farming and may have dealt Tiwanaku a fatal blow.

5

The Central Andes
of South America:
Late Civilizations and the Inca

Fall and Transformation on the North Coast

The cultures of the period A.D. 100 to 600 had brought to maturity the religious, political, social, and economic structures developed during the preceding three thousand years. However, as a result of a series of natural disasters, things began to fall apart beginning about the mid-sixth century. El Niño episodes occurred in A.D. 546 and 576, but even so a thirty-two-year drought of Old Testament proportions that began in A.D. 562 probably "dried the well" in the case of the Moche. El Niño brought floods, devastating erosion, and partial washouts of the life-giving irrigation systems. Earthquakes also occurred and tilted the systems so that the carefully calculated gradients no long worked. These calamities resulted in famine and an increase in diseases, aggravating the miseries of the already stricken populations. In turn, these misfortunes led to the downfall of the elites supported by those populations (Moseley 1992:209–212). The noble courts that had existed in each of the major Moche valleys apparently fell into disrepute and in some cases were held responsible by their people for the disasters. The main capital at Cerro Blanco (Moche Valley) was abandoned. A new capital, Pampa Grande, was established in the Lambayeque Valley, away from the some of the worst effects of the natural catastrophes, and yet it lasted only a century and was also beset by floods and abandoned by A.D. 750. The city was burned at the end, and yet another new center established under new leadership. This change led to the eventual revitalization of the North Coast, but first we must examine a remarkable empire that was built at this time with its capital in the Central Highlands.

The Huari Empire

A large ruin near the present-day city of Ayacucho, Peru, has impressed travelers for centuries. Huge walls outline about seventy-five large compounds, within which are the remains of two- and three-story buildings. This is the city of Huari, which was established about A.D. 600 and which dominated a large-scale empire in the Central and Northern Highlands and in some parts of the adjacent coast for about four hundred years. The origins of this dynamic state are imperfectly known. Prior to about A.D. 550, the region apparently had no state-level societies and no sophisticated temple centers. Each ethnic group of the area appears to have had its own main community. Isbell (1988) thinks that the decentralized and difficult irrigation problems of the region led, paradoxically, to the formation of a highly centralized state system. The process appears to have worked as follows. Each small community or group of communities had its own water sources for watering hillside terrace systems. These were marginal to the main food production system, which was located on the valley floors. Nevertheless, the long drought combined with an already risky climatic regime of late and irregular rainfall to produce a food crisis. The once marginal irrigation systems then became the mainstay of agriculture in the Huari region. However, expansion of these systems was complex and delicate and required constant attention and maintenance. The systems also required overall coordination and management. The appearance of the state in the Huari region was therefore rapid, rationalized, and probably a response to conflict among the irrigation groups (Isbell 1987). In addition, Huari also appears to have invented a system of labor allocation and production that was adopted by the later Inca. Among the Inca, labor by groups was paid for by housing the workers in quarters similar to barracks and by feeding and supplying them in other ways. Large barracks, kitchens, and storehouses are all required by such a system, and the major Huari centers possess these features.

Tiwanaku may have been involved, either by furnishing an example of state organization or by furnishing the leadership itself. That ancient center also furnished the ideological glue for the new empire. The sun god of Tiwanaku was transformed at Huari into a Front Face Deity who holds staffs in both hands. Smaller attendants with wings often run toward the god at the center of a sculpture or textile. This set of motifs was widely spread over the Andes in all the zones controlled and influenced by Huari.

At A.D. 700 Huari had a population of about twenty-five thousand sustained by mountain terrace and irrigation systems of complex and ingenious design (Isbell and Schreiber 1978; Isbell 1987; Isbell 1988). Its zone of influence reached over a vast area—700 km (435 miles) north to the large administrative center of Viracochapampa and beyond, as shown by Huari-influenced pottery in graves as far away as Ecuador. Another center was located 230 km (143 miles) to the southeast. Both centers have large compounds similar to those at Huari and probably were tied to it by a net of roads. These highways preceded and possibly were the model for the famous Inca road system. An intrusion into the Moquegua Valley on the South Coast occurred when people from the highlands began to settle there in the period after the beginning of the drought. The Nazca Valley was also occupied by Huari colonists. Military muscle was apparently applied during the colonization process, judging by the presence of a Huari fortress (Cerro Baul) located on a butte in the Moquegua (Moseley 1992:221).

Huari was a successful empire-building state, using diplomacy, trade, intimidation, ideology, and militarism in a classic combination. Its end around A.D. 1250 is less well understood. Schreiber suggests that it existed on accumulated capital confiscated by force from other regions. Therefore, when it ceased to expand, it collapsed. Huari's continued expansion was probably blocked by strong states to its north and south (Schreiber 1988:96).

The Chimu Kingdom and Chan Chan

The Chimu state was another desert kingdom on the North Coast, more or less covering the same territory anciently controlled by the Moche state. However, the agricultural base of the Chimu was considerably less than the irrigated land cultivated by the Moche. Tilting, earthquakes, and uplift activity had literally thrown the systems off their designed gradients, and water would not flow in some of the altered ditches and canals. The periodic El Niño episodes that plagued the Moche had also taken their toll in washed-out irrigation systems and eroded growing surfaces. In spite of all those problems, even on the lowest social levels Chimu nutrition was sufficient and even good.

The Chimu rulers governed from the capital city of Chan Chan (see Figure 5.1). The ruins of this city in the Moche Valley have attracted the attention of travelers for centuries because of the massive adobe walls decorated with animal, fish, and bird designs. The city and the state were established about A.D. 1000. From this capital the kingdom of Chimor (its ancient name) eventually expanded south to the Rimac Valley (close to the vicinity of modern Lima) and north to the Gulf of Guayaquil along about 1,000 km (ca. 620 miles) of coast. The kingdom lasted for about 470 years before the even greater and more aggressive Inca conquered the Chimu. Chan Chan was oriented around ten large precincts, each surrounded by decorated adobe walls more than 9 m (up to 30 feet) high. Each enclosure was built by a successive ruler, of whom ten are listed in Spanish colonial chronicles. These compounds varied in size from 88,000 to 221,000 m^2 (172,000 to 433,000 feet^2). Thus in each reign the city grew by means of massive construction projects driven by the need for supporting nobility and commoners. Inside each enclosure was a palace with offices and storerooms as well as a burial place for the king. Offices were in the form of audience rooms *(audiencias)* with platforms on which officials sat to meet with others and to receive tribute from various groups. The tribute, in the form of food, textiles, and manufactured items, was stored in a great number of rooms nearby.

The reason for the construction of a new palace establishment for each new king lies in a custom called split inheritance. Under this principle, the ruler inherited power and offices but no material wealth. All the preceding king's wealth was left to secondary heirs who formed a corporation that took care of the ritual of memorialization of the dead ruler. These heirs were supported by the old king's wealth. The new king was therefore forced to increase taxes (labor, goods) or to conquer new territories that would pay tribute. This process led to constant expansion of the Chimu state but also of the headquarters and capital city. This rule of inheritance was adopted by the later Inca.

When a king of Chimor died he was buried in a T-shaped chamber in a large platform adjacent to his palace. Large-scale human sacrifice of young men (two to three hundred at a time) was practiced in order that the king might have his attendants in afterlife as on earth. All royal Chimu burials were looted in colonial or modern times, but remains of fine textiles, carved wood, jewelry, excellent pottery, and other indicators of great wealth have been found around the tombs. Llamas were also sac-

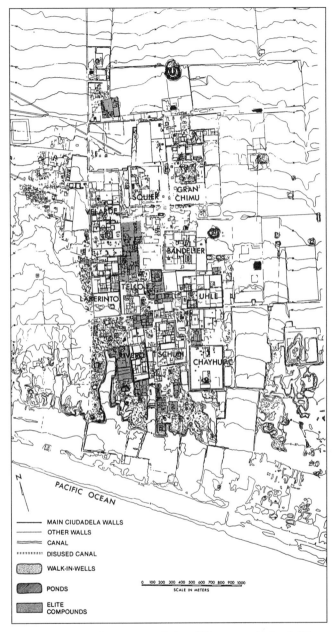

FIGURE 5.1   Site map of the Chimu capital of Chan Chan, Peru. (Courtesy of Michael E. Moseley.)

rificed and buried near the king. The secondary heirs made periodic offerings and sacrifices (including humans) to the dead ruler.

The palaces must have been sumptuous and magnificent. They were furnished with textiles and cushions and decorated with friezes and paintings. The labyrinthine series of courtyards, offices, storerooms, and corridors was guarded by porters, soldiers, and bureaucrats. Secrecy, privacy, and a vast social gulf between nobility and commoners are implied by these extraordinary buildings.

The lower nobility lived in compounds near the royal enclosures. Eventually there were thirty-five of these, each probably representing an aristocratic household. Four *huacas* (platforms) were located at Chan Chan, and these were probably burial places for nonroyal nobility.

About twenty thousand people lived in large numbers of small apartments that give the impression of bee hives. These were the homes of artisans and other palace workers. Storerooms, audience rooms, and workshops are located in and around the residences. Four social classes lived and worked in these apartments and workshops. Some of them ate very well, consuming llamas and guinea pigs as well as sea birds. At least some of this food and other supplies supporting these urban workers came from the storerooms of the palaces and therefore from the commodities collected as taxes (S. Pozorski 1982).

The farmers in the villages also ate well, although they undoubtedly worked very hard. One village depended largely on irrigated field crops (beans, for example) that they themselves raised as well as on llamas and seafoods. They raised and contributed a variety of foodstuffs to the urban population of Chan Chan, including maize, common beans, squashes, gourds, cotton, peanuts, aji (pepper), and fruits from five kinds of orchard trees. Another farming community operated a system known as sunken gardens, in which large areas were dug down to groundwater level and crops were raised in the lowered and moist soils. These people lived in houses made of cane and thatch on top of the mounds of earth excavated from the gardens. They ate relatively well, with two-thirds of their animal protein from the sea and most of the rest from llamas. Lower on the social and economic scale was a group of road and cemetery laborers who lived near their work areas. This group ate both less often and less well. All of their animal protein came from seafoods (S. Pozorski 1982).

Early on, the Chimu launched a series of massive reclamation projects that mainly took the form of extending the older Moche irrigation systems. The landscape was transformed by the integration of canals, field walls, and roads, all carefully and centrally planned. An extraordinary attempt was made to bring water from the neighboring Chicama Valley to the Moche Valley by means of the Intervalley Canal, begun about A.D. 1200 and under construction for nearly two hundred years. The project was abandoned in about A.D. 1400. The southern end of the canal had risen as a result of tectonic movements, and water would not flow through the channel. In fact, nearly all Chimu expansions of canal systems show that they were eventually abandoned, probably for the same reason: the gradual but inexorable uplift and tilting of land surfaces along the Peruvian coast (Nials et al. 1979; Ortloff, Moseley, and Feldman 1982). Catastrophic floods from a particularly severe El Niño in A.D. 1100 also contributed to the difficulty of maintaining food production. Moreover, the episode also weakened an independent northern dynasty in the Lambayeque Valley, where the enraged population threw its ruler, Fempellec, into the sea for having "caused" the floods by an act of impiety (Moseley 1992:250, 254). The Chimu later expanded into this area and even farther north into what is now southern Ecuador. In contrast to what happened to their predecessors, ecological difficulties and catastrophic events did not bring an end to the Chimu culture. It adjusted each time and continued in a new adaptation. Instead, it was a more powerful culture arising in the highlands that destroyed both the Chimu and the indigenous North Coast cultural tradition.

We have now reached the stage at which the Andean civilizations were united for a last period under a grand and coherent philosophy of statehood and economic integration represented by the Inca empire.

Inca Civilization

Historical Features

We and our ancestors in Western civilization down the centuries have heard tales of Inca splendor and of an imperial state that stretched over mountain ranges, coastal deserts, and perhaps into the Amazonian fringes. Many of the fabulous rumors or embellishments are wrong, but still manage to convey the amazement of the Spaniards at what they saw. Some information was recorded imperfectly by eyewitnesses and later by historians who worked with native traditions. Modern scholars have sifted these sources and checked them against the material remains of archaeology, and we now probably understand the Inca better than any westerners since the first, mostly illiterate Spanish conquerors. What follows is still derived largely from ethnohistoric studies (particularly those of John Rowe), supplemented with ethnographic research and complemented by recent archaeological research.

The Inca name for their empire was Tahuantinsuyu, or Four Quarters of the World. However, the Inca were not always the overshadowing culture that they became after 1428. Before that time, they were a small and unnoticed group in the Central Highlands in the area of Cuzco. That city later became the capital of the empire, and subsequently was the Spanish colonial capital. As a result, the earliest remains of Inca culture are buried under the modern, colonial, and Inca city. Some carelessly decorated but serviceable pottery that dates to about A.D. 1200 represents the earliest cultural remains. For 250 years the Inca occupied their section of the Central Andes, doing highland agriculture, herding llamas and guanacos, and living in dispersed villages that were dominated by the *ayllu* kinship unit.

The later Inca traced their ancestry back to a sacred island on Lake Titicaca, although this is probably a myth produced for purposes of greater prestige. By about A.D. 1438, the Inca were under pressure from several competing groups, especially one called the Chanca to the northwest. These people had conquered neighbors of the Inca, the Quechua, and were preparing to attack the Inca. The aged Inca (ruler) and his principal heir fled to a distant fort for safety in the face of this threat. Another son successfully led the Inca resistance to the Chanca invasion forces, saved Cuzco, and then usurped the throne from his brother. This was the first emperor, Pachacuti, who, assisted by his son Topa Inca, went on to conquer vast areas of the Andes both north and south of Cuzco. Topa Inca made an end run around the coastal Chimu kingdom and came down from the north, achieving strategic and tactical surprise and success.

Pachacuti began, in the style of many great conquerors, to remake the capital city of Cuzco. The urban plan was in the form of a great puma, and sacred lines *(ceques)* oriented *huacas* and temples in and around the city. Cuzco became a splendid metropolis with lavishly decorated public buildings, palaces, and storehouses. Reorganization did not stop with the capital, however, and Pachacuti also set up the various state mechanisms and vast public works that made the Inca such an object of wonder to later generations. One of these was the identification of the Inca with the sun god Inti, who became the patron of Cuzco. The famous Sun Temple, whose foundations can still be seen, was built in his honor. Pachacuti established a far-reaching bureaucracy (to be discussed in a later section), rationalized taxation and storage of food and other goods, and began and expanded a communication system based on a network of roads. Meanwhile Topa Inca continued on his conquests, finally ascending to the throne upon his father's death in 1471. His heir, Huayna Capac, expanded the realm, but his reign was cut short by his premature death, probably from smallpox, which had spread from Mexico through Central America and into the Andes by this time. His death led to a civil war between the survivors of the ruling house, won at last by Atahualpa, who himself was almost immediately met, kidnapped, ransomed, betrayed, and killed by the murderous Spanish conquerors in A.D. 1532.

Social Organization

The kinship unit called the *ayllu,* discussed in Chapter 4, was the basis for society and was incorporated into the later Inca state as an administrative unit. The *ayllu* was a group of families who were related through both male and female lines of descent from a common ancestor. The *ayllus* were divided into two parts, technically called moieties. Marriage was only permissible between men and women of different moieties, but one could not marry outside the *ayllu.* In other words, one married within the larger social group but outside the subdivision to which one belonged. The effect was to make the *ayllu* an autonomous work and reproductive unit. As Moseley points out, individual families could not hope to be independent in Andean farming. Therefore the *ayllu* was also the basic economic unit, owning and managing land and water systems. This kin, economic, social, work unit was fundamental to all groups in the area and probably had a long history prior to the Inca period. However, by no means were all the *ayllus* equal in resources, and wealth varied from the level of individual couples up through the *ayllus* themselves. All persons in Inca society were concerned with their ancestors, who had given them their rights, statuses, and roles. The practices of wrapping the bodies of the ancestors, of mummification, and of family tombs that we have seen in the ancient past reflect a long standing-focus on forebears. Extended families preferred to live in enclosures with three to six houses. Such enclosures are found at Machu Picchu and other Inca period sites. Leadership was exercised by consensus of lineage leaders within the *ayllu* and by the two moiety leaders, the *karakas.* The *karakas* formed a lower nobility. The term *ayllu* also referred to eleven royal lineages, now extinct, of course. *Ayllus* still operate in the modern Andes, although some functions and features have changed (Rowe 1946; Moseley 1992:49–51).

Political and Economic Structures

The Tahuantinsuyu was, not surprisingly, divided into four segments. Each of these quarters was, in turn, divided into provinces ruled by a governor. Provinces roughly corresponded to the ethnic groups and the formerly independent states conquered or annexed by the empire. Each province was divided into two sections (moieties again) unless they were very populous; if so, a third section was added. The sections were divided into *ayllus,* a structural feature that effectively integrated the political and the kinship systems. An upper group of aristocrats was made up of the descendants of rulers. These royal nobles filled the upper levels of government, including the governorships. The *karakas* reported to the governors and were themselves organized into a decimal system with chiefs of 10,000 taxpayers, then of 5,000, 1,000, 500, and 100. Foremen supervised groups of 50 and 10 taxpayers. A continuing and annually corrected census kept in Cuzco allowed management of taxation and military service. The information was recorded on the famous bundles of knotted and colored strings, the *quipus.* The *quipu* system sets the Andes and the Inca in particular apart from other early world civilizations in that the Inca lacked a true writing system.

Taxation was by labor. This simple statement nonetheless summarizes the basis of state revenues for the Inca. Agricultural lands were worked by both men and women and were divided into three classes. One portion was set aside for the government, another for the gods and religion, and a third part to sustain the people. Government and religious (temple and other institutions) lands were cultivated first, but each family was allotted enough through the *ayllu* to keep it comfortably fed. A labor tax also was levied on textiles, under which both men and women were required to weave for a certain portion of time for the state with materials provided to them. Another form of labor taxation was known as *mita;* this was the obligation on the part of males to work on roads, irrigation, agricultural terraces, construction projects, and other state projects. Millions toiled in the service of the state and gods, and the results are still a matter of awe. John Hyslop (1990) points out that through the expansion of the agricultural terracing, the Inca converted an ephemeral form of wealth, labor, into food-producing land. Certain districts were exempt from *mita* service but provided special services or materials to the state. The Rucana district, for example, supplied litter bearers.

The importance of cloth to Andean cultures has been noted from early times. Among the Inca, it was the preferred gift and ceremonial item and an indicator of status in a way that few cultures have used it. The major fibers were llama wool in the highlands and cotton on the coast. The finest fabrics were naturally reserved for the rulers and nobility, whereas commoners wore rough material. One of the privileges of *karakas* was their access to cloth. Large numbers of the storehouses around and in Inca administrative centers were stuffed with raw wool, cotton, cloth, and garments. The army used large quantities of clothes, blankets, and tents (Murra 1962). Altogether, the emphasis on fabrics as a status symbol and as a preeminently valued commodity is unique to the Andean area.

Huge amounts of foodstuffs, manufactured goods, and materials were accumulated by the state and stored away in special buildings. *Karaka* officials were authorized to distribute these supplies to their people in cases of disasters such as crop failures or earthquakes. Supplies were also built up in this manner for military campaigns. Weapons dumps were maintained in the administrative centers and in certain of the state roadside inns. The state revenues and surpluses were immense, so that the effects of natural or other catastrophes were probably better dealt with than in modern times. In the civil wars among the Spanish and Inca factions that followed the initial Spanish conquest, these large and widely distributed supplies were used for the various armies. In fact, some scholars argue that the civil wars only came to an end after ten years when the stored materials ran out (Rowe 1946:280).

The Inca Road System

Perhaps the best-known aspect of Inca civilization is that they built a huge and complex road network (see Map 5.1). What is less commonly known is that although the system included many sections that predated the Inca, the entire network was completed in less than ninety years. The true extent and details of this huge public work are still not completely known, in spite of a number of dedicated researchers and especially the excellent work of John Hyslop (1984). He comments that the empire surely created the road system but that the system also made the vast empire possible.

Eventually a system of roads reached from Quito, Ecuador, down to Santiago, Chile, a distance of about 5,630 km (3,500 miles). The total

MAP 5.1   The Inca empire

mileage now mapped is about 22,530 km (14,000 miles), and Hyslop (1984) thinks that the total system was once more than 40,233 km (25,000 aggregate miles). This is a stupendous achievement for a civilization that had very few mechanical aids. The roads were far from uniform. In the Sechura Desert of the North Coast and the Atacama Desert to the south, the road consisted only of large posts in a long line across the wastes. Mountain secondary roads were only 1.2 to 1.8 m (4 to 6 feet) wide and scarcely more than regularized footpaths. Main routes, however, were about 10.6 m (35 feet) wide. In some steep mountain terrains, the road became a series of broad staircases. In the marshy zones along the edges of lakes, especially Lake Titicaca, causeways with culverts were built. Bridging was ingenious and varied, and the suspension bridges are famous. The great rope bridge over the Apurimac River spanned nearly 46 m (150 feet). Many smaller fiber bridges were also used, all of them apparently stabilized against the winds with guy ropes. Wooden and stone bridges were used where possible. In some cases in the rugged terrain it was impracticable to build permanent bridges, and so reed pontoon bridges and ferries were installed.

Mita (taxation) labor built, maintained, and operated the road system and the *tampus*, a system of about two thousand state inns, each located a day's journey apart. Nearby communities were also expected to stock these establishments with food, firewood, and even clothing, arms, and other supplies. The use of *tampus* was restricted to state travelers. In some isolated and thinly populated zones, the *tampu* was also the administrative headquarters. Vast quantities of state-owned materials were accumulated in storehouses that were a feature of the *tampus*.

Rates of travel were rapid, considering the immense distances and rugged topography. Present-day Andean natives often travel 50 km (31 miles) per day, walking singly or in small parties. The pattern of intermittent walking and running used in the Andes reminds one of a similar system used by the rapidly moving rifle companies of the eighteenth-century British army. Present-day native Andean travelers move at night as well as in daytime. High officials, including the Inca, were carried in litters, with relays of carriers shifting the burden at short intervals. On one coastal road, there are three lanes, of which the center was reserved for the Inca himself and high state officials.

The relay runner-messenger *(chaski)* system was also remarkable. Thousands of men relayed messages and small objects over great distances in short times. The distance between runners was highly variable, about 8

km (5 miles) on flat ground and perhaps 1.6 km (1 mile) in steep mountains. The runner system was operative twenty-four hours a day, making it
possible to pass a message and the data recorded on *quipus* from one end
of the empire to the other in a matter of days. Messages were short and
summary and repeated by each runner several times to avoid confused
transmission. Service as a *chaski* runner was a *mita* obligation.

Religion

To the Inca, nearly every aspect of nature was sacred, although there was a
definite scale of importance in the supernatural universe just as on earth.
At the top of creation was the author of the cosmos, Viracocha, the most
abstract deity and one whose worship was largely confined to the upper
classes. The cult was very old, however, and was widespread throughout
the Central Andes. Brian Bauer points out that the creation cult was also
connected to one of the most pervasive Andean religious beliefs, that of
natural origin places for the *ayllus*. Each *ayllu* had a separate origin point,
which might be a stone, spring, river, cave, or even trees and herbs, from
which it was descended. These origin points were called *huacas* but also
paqarisqas, or "creators of their natures" (Bauer 1991:8–9). Although not
the only *huacas*, these were the most important of these sacred locations;
because there were hundreds of *ayllus*, this status partly accounts for the
great number of *huacas*.

   The Inca had seized upon the sun god Inti as their special and patron
deity. The sun was the origin and progenitor of the royal *ayllus* and the
ruler himself. Sun temples were established throughout the empire, and
the most important temple, named Coricancha, was located in the capital
of Cuzco. From the great gold-adorned building radiated a series of 41 sacred lines *(ceques)* along which were 328 *huacas*, or sacred spots, in the valley around Cuzco. The lines divided the city, the empire, and the universe
into four quarters, and each of these, in turn, was complexly subdivided.
About one-third of the *huacas* around were associated with water sources,
and in fact the worship of water, water sources, and the thunder god (Il-
lapa) was only subordinate to the worship of the sun and the creator god.
The earth was surrounded by and lay above water. Therefore, drains,
fountains, baths, and libations were all religiously important (as was the
case with the water channels through the early temple at Chavin de
Huantar). A series of sixteen fountains descend a slope at Machu Picchu,
the well-known Inca hilltop fastness in the Cuzco region (Hyslop

1990:129–145). The second capital of the empire, Tomebamba (Cuenca, Ecuador), had a spectacular Sun Temple that was bracketed by water channels in the same manner as was the central section of Cuzco.

From the highest nobility to the lowest *ayllu* member in the Inca empire, however, perhaps the most pervasive religious theme was that of ancestor veneration or worship (Conrad and Demarest 1984:116). The Inca cared for royal ancestor mummies, conversed with them, and paraded them in public on great occasions; the mummies were ultimately the justification of the rulers' status and power. *Ayllu* ancestors were also venerated and memorialized with ritual and sacrifices. This concept can be seen deep in the past and was widely spread. The Paracas mummies, the royal tombs in the great Moche platforms, and the Chimu retainer burials of kings all are related to this fundamental concept of Andean religion.

Sacrifice is nearly universal in religions. The higher nobility sacrificed llamas, textiles, *chicha* (corn beer), and many precious objects. Human sacrifices have been noted numerous times in the preceding review of more ancient cultures in the Andes. The Inca carried on the practice but did not expand it. People of lower estate and perhaps even impoverished people offered what they had, sometimes being reduced to offering hair from eyebrows or eyelashes (Mason 1968:216).

By laying out their cities and centers in cosmic diagrams, the Inca accomplished several purposes. They constantly reminded non-Inca peoples of the Inca view of the world. By the incorporation of rocks, sacred water, lines of shrines, clusters of temples, alignment on mountains, and other devices, the Inca also integrated their architecture into what Hyslop has called their "animate, sacred landscape" (1990:305). They reproduced parts or all of the basic cosmological outlines of Cuzco as well.

The Armies

Soldiers were equipped with helmets, quilted cotton armor, shields, and personal weapons. Combat was both (relatively) long range and at close quarters. Slings and spear throwers were used by specialists who inflicted damage on the enemy by clouds of missiles. Bows and arrows were used only by Inca army units recruited from the Amazon slopes and tropical lowlands. Fortresses were defended by rolling large rocks down on the enemy. Clubs with six-pointed heads were the favorite hand-to-hand weapon, the mace heads being made of varying materials dependent upon the status of the warrior. Battle axes, long thrusting spears, and sword-shaped clubs made up the rest of the weapons system. It is noteworthy that the Inca made no use of siege engines. However, the weapons used were very effective in the context of armies without cavalry (no horses), firearms (no gunpowder), or wheeled vehicles. Trophies consisted of the heads of dangerous enemies and even their stuffed skins at times. Occasionally, drums were made from the skin of an enemy as well, or flutes were made from their shin bones (Rowe 1946:274–280).

Tactics were simple. It was a matter of bringing the army to grips with the enemy, intimidating them with the numbers of the Inca army and the suddenness of their appearance, and then moving to contact as rapidly as possible. Although march discipline was strict, battlefield discipline was loose, and formations broke apart when battle was joined. A battle therefore was even more the sum of individual combats than in other armies. Very little control could be exercised by commanders under these circumstances. Strategic moves, such as that of sweeping down from the north upon the Chimu, made up for some of this lack of tactical finesse. However, these failings became fatal when the Inca confronted the Spanish armies on the field of battle. Logistics, in contrast, were superbly handled. The army could be reequipped on the march from the vast stores of supplies and equipment along the roads. Movement was rapid, thanks to the road system.

Cities, Administrative Centers, and Fortresses

Although the Inca made Cuzco their capital, it had apparently existed for centuries as a non-Inca community. Located at an altitude of about 3,566 m (11,700 feet) above sea level and with three streams running through it, Cuzco had some special site problems to resolve. The city was rebuilt after the Inca had overcome their immediate enemies in the wars of 1428. Unfortunately for archaeologists, the city was burned in the Inca revolt of 1535, and the Spaniards also destroyed a great many of the original buildings in the construction of their own colonial capital. Surprisingly, not very much archaeology has been done within modern Cuzco, and therefore we must rely on general impressions and descriptions of people who lived in Cuzco in the early and mid-sixteenth century.

The capital of Cuzco was built in the form of a puma, with the great fortress Sacsahuaman forming the head of the cosmic beast. This plan and the influence of other religious conceptions on urban layout was also reflected by the *ceque* system already mentioned. The Sun Temple (Qori Cancha) was near the center of the city. The city had a large central plaza that was divided into two parts by one of the rivers. The dual plaza corresponded to the two divisions of royal *ayllus*. Near the center of the plaza was a carved stone altar-throne used in ceremonies by the Inca ruler. Around the plaza were several large and important buildings. One was the residence of the "chosen women" of the sun, who were somewhat like members of Christian religious orders—their lives dedicated to work and service. Palaces of the current and past rulers of the empire occupied part of the area. These and many other buildings in Cuzco were made in two styles of impressively fine stonework. The great halls mentioned in the epigraph at the beginning of Chapter 1 were also on one side of the dual plaza. These may have been used for feasts and other ceremonies. Away from the center of the city were a great many private houses, perhaps sufficient to shelter as many as 100,000 people. It is impossible to accurately locate the other features of the ancient city without some careful archaeological digging. Undoubtedly most people lived in housing arranged in *cancha* (courtyard) groups. We are also told by the chroniclers that there were a jail, botanical gardens, small plazas, extensive storage facilities, schools, *tampus*, and other amenities (Hyslop 1990:43).

Although the function has been disputed recently (Hyslop 1990:43), every Spanish eyewitness who saw the immense hilltop structure of Sacsahuaman described it as a fortress with an emphasis on its military function. It is one of the few ancient structures visible in and around Cuzco that gives an idea of its original form. The hill on which the fortress is built has three massive terrace walls designed in a zigzag plan to make assault more difficult. Gigantic blocks of stone, carefully fitted together, have amazed generations of travelers and archaeologists. On the top of the hill were a number of large buildings, including two towers, one of which was at least four stories high. Excavations have revealed the foundations of the towers and the remains of cisterns, staircases, many rooms, and other features. The eyewitness account adds that the fortress could shelter five thousand people and that in it were stored a large quantity of arms and military equipment. A smaller terraced hill lies opposite the larger, and a sizable leveled plaza lies between them.

Beyond the main city lay estates of regional lords and housing for workers doing their service to the state and for craftsmen and artisans of various kinds. The regional lords were required to reside at the capital for part of the year and therefore required elaborate establishments in the vicinity. A ring of ethnic settlements lay around Cuzco, with the populations usually attached to their lord.

According to the latest research of Rowe (in Bruhns 1994:334) and his students, the famous mountaintop site of Machu Picchu was the royal estate of the emperor Pachacuti. Its location was concealed for centuries until Hiram Bingham discovered it in 1911, on its ridge above the Urubamba River, surrounded by towering mountains. Terraces and buildings alternate. The top of the ridge was leveled for a plaza around which several large buildings are set. Houses spill down the ridge slope on dozens of terraces. At least ten carved outcroppings of rock, the water fountains, and the shrines on the Inca road approaching it indicate that Machu Picchu had more of a religious function than had been thought (Hyslop 1990:112). However, it was also a fastness set in a highly defensible position.

An Inca city in the north highlands, Huanuco Pampa, was set in an extraordinary location 3,657 m (12,000 feet) above sea level (see Figure 5.2). The center has been well studied recently and is probably the best preserved of Inca cities outside of Cuzco (Morris and Thompson 1985). Huanuco Pampa is situated where it is because of the Inca road that passes through this high, rolling plain on the way to Tomebamba (Cuenca). The city is thoroughly integrated into the road network, and there are *tampus* a day's journey to the south and north of it. The plain also served as pasture for the alpaca herds maintained for their wool. The Inca selected the site for these reasons and also as an administrative center for the newly conquered region. They began construction about 1460 and were still building in 1532. A very large temple stands unfinished, with large stones scattered across the prairie where they were abandoned on the way from the quarry.

The city includes over 3,500 buildings arranged in four quarters around a huge plaza. A platform of Cuzco-style masonry stands in the center of the plaza for ceremonies and reviews. This was the equivalent of the sacred stone in the center of the plazas of Cuzco. Each quarter of the city is divided into three parts, making a total of twelve, as in Cuzco. On the north side of the plaza is a compound for "chosen women" *(aklla),* whose primary duties at the city were to make beer for feasts and cloth as well. *Mita* workers resided in a compound that has a number of barracks in it. It is calculated that ten to fifteen thousand people could be housed in the city. A residence for the governor and/or for the Inca on his rare visits is located in the extreme eastern quarter and is much more finely built than most other structures at the site. An early chronicler mentions Huanuco Pampa as one of a group of "other Cuzcos," which is to say that the cities

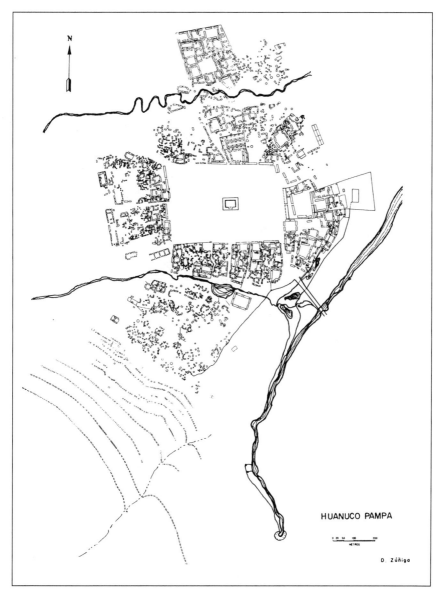

FIGURE 5.2   Site map of the Inca administrative center of Huanuco Pampa.
(Courtesy of Craig Morris.)

were laid out with the same cosmic principles in mind. Another early writer says that maize grown at lower altitudes was brought to Huanuco Pampa, seven days journey away, and that coca leaf was brought from the Amazonian slopes of the Andes by means of a nine-day journey. Huge amounts of maize, potatoes, and cloth were stored at the city in special storehouses. Although the city was far removed from most food sources, it was secured from famine by the stored resources. There are over 35,000 cubic meters (45,780 cubic yards) of storage space.

Thompson, Morris, and Murra explored the various villages of different ethnic groups mentioned as residing in the region and found that they all maintained their traditional architecture and pottery and even village locations. The Inca intruded into their region by means of the road system and with a new level of governance. Huanuco Pampa was the manifestation of the empire. The city was the center of feasting and the source of gifts of cloth and other materials. These rituals were used by the Inca to politically integrate varied ethnic groups into the imperial structure. As Morris and Thompson (1985) point out, it was a fragile way in which to assure political loyalty and made the imperial system vulnerable to the ruthless and driving ambition of the Spanish conquerors.

*   *   *

> Next day the Spaniards entered Cuzco without any resistance, and at once some began to pull down the walls of the temple which were of gold and silver, others to dig up the jewels and jars of gold that had been buried with the dead, and still others to seize idols made of the same metal. They also sacked the houses and the fortress, which still contained much gold from the time of [Huayna Capac]. . . . The Spaniards were not satisfied with what they had, but wearied the Indians by digging everything up and turning it inside out, and treated them very badly, committing many cruelties to get them to talk about the treasure and show them tombs. (Lopez de Gomara, quoted in Garcilaso de la Vega 1966:748–749)

Epilogue

Several parallels and contrasts have probably struck the reader in considering the culture histories and evolutionary features of the earliest civilizations. One is certainly the matter of scale. Numbers of people and the size and nature of the landscape they occupy have something to do with the cultural structures as well as general ethos of civilized societies. Table 1 presents a rough comparison of the geographic extents of all six pristine civilizations. Of all the early complex cultures, Egypt was probably the one most unchanged through time, retaining its identity from about 3000 to 330 B.C. It also encompassed the smallest and most ecologically restricted area. Perhaps, when the basic problems of large-scale food production, formation of state structures, and meeting religious needs were solved in Egypt, it was less stressful to have done with experimentation. Certainly, the later experiments of the Heretic Pharaoh Iknahton were not well received, and it was really only when the purifying and purgative effects of Islamic proselytization struck Egypt in the ninth century A.D. that most of the older structures were finally discarded or modified. Resistance to change, of course, was not confined to Egypt. China, occupying the largest and probably the most ecologically diverse area, became extraordinarily conservative. However, the effect was delayed until the development of the Confucian bureaucratic literati, and the political (and cultural) unification of China was also much later than in Egypt. Both lags in China were probably a function of the difference in scale.

In the New World, political unification of a whole culture area took place only in the Central Andes. The Inca also homogenized the Andean cultures in a way that did not occur in Mesoamerica. In Mesoamerica, imperial structures were built on a much more fragile political base. In fact, one could argue that the Teotihuacan, Toltec, and Aztec imperial ventures were ultimately vast extensions of their city-state capitals. Likewise, in contrast to the situation in the Andes, none of the three Meosamerican empires tried to culturally integrate subject peoples in the way that the

TABLE 1   Relative Geographical Sizes of World Pristine Civilizations

Culture Areas	Area in Square Kilometers	Area in Square Miles
China	3,885,000	1,500,000
Middle East	1,500,000	597,000
Mesoamerica	1,000,000	397,000
Central Andes	926,000	357,000
Indus Valley	80,000	30,888
Nile Valley	34,000	13,127

Inca did. In this regard, the Inca appear to be the New World culture closest to that of traditional China.

In Chapter 1 I pointed out some detailed resemblances among the world's earliest civilizations. It should be emphasized that, aside from Egypt and the Near East, none of the civilized areas was in contact with the others. Therefore many of these similarities may be functionally necessary features that are needed by any human group that develops complex culture. However, it should also be emphasized that these commonalities are not inevitable, as was suggested by Marx and other theorists. When one examines the nature of the institution closely in each case, it is found that writing, for example, is stylistically and even operationally distinct. It is the function served by a similar mechanism or cultural institution. To take another example, state-level societies and their administrative arrangements vary wildly from area to area and yet serve the same political and bureaucratic functions. In other words, humanity's infinite cultural inventiveness is apparent in detail and even in gross features. However, even with these caveats, similarities are striking.

Parallels are even more interesting in the several evolutionary histories and the dynamics that operated to produce the comparable forms of religion, politics, writing, urban life, trade, and other aspects of civilized life. Several active elements have been noted in the examination of many of the complex cultures of the Old and New Worlds. These features include population growth, conflict, cooperation (forced or voluntary), interaction among cultures through trade, and integration through warfare, religion, and political systems. These are best illustrated in detail and have been the subject of many books.

An observation that seems to have more than passing interest is that all the cultural developments described in this book came from what are called archaic societies. That is, the major basis for social organization, political leadership, religious life, and other matters largely rested upon kinship groups and tribal associations. These were often amalgamated into a state-level society such as that of the Aztecs. Ancestor reverence in the Chinese, Maya, and Inca cases was a powerful integrative feature. However, emphasis on kinship and small ethnic groups can be disruptive to a larger political system, as is the case in the Balkans historically and presently. The Inca attempted to eliminate this disruptive feature by the isolation of and moving of clan groups.

The breakdown of large political systems, whether they were regional states or empires, appears to have allowed nobility to grasp additional power and land in the same way as happened in the late Roman empire. This resulted in a kind of generalized feudalism wherever in the world it occurred. For example, with the breakdown of centralized authority in the Maya Late Classic states, local lords moved onto the land with client farm and artisan families living near their country residences.

The complex cultures of the New World got off to late starts compared to those in the Old World. One can only speculate that the New World may have been handicapped by the relative lack of grains and animals suitable for domestication. This meant that New World cultures had to painfully develop a series of difficult plants over much longer periods of time than in the Old World, and therefore the economic basis for civilization was not possible until about 2000 B.C. in South America and 1500 B.C. in Mesoamerica, compared to 6500 B.C. in the Near East, for example.

One must wonder what forms New World cultures might have assumed if they had been allowed to evolve for another thousand years. The abrupt truncation of development in the Andes and Mesoamerica finished off these areas in terms not only of cultural forms but also of human populations. For, as Murdo MacLeod (1973) has characterized it, the Spanish conquests of Peru and Mexico were not just military matters but were also a War of the Worlds, to use the title of H. G. Wells's famous story. European diseases eliminated the population basis for further development, even had the controlling native elites survived the European conquests. Within 160 years after the conquest of Mexico, for example, it is estimated that 90 to 95 percent of the native populations had died. It is argued that this created an economic depression in the seventeenth century and inhibited the development of culturally integrated societies in what is now Latin America.

Although the linkages between present-day Latin American societies and their pre-Columbian predecessors are indirect and often tenuous, such linkages represent a considerable cultural heritage for many peoples.

The indigenous groups of Peru, Bolivia, Guatemala, Mexico, Belize, and elsewhere are awakening to the achievements of their ancestors and claiming the rich past as their own. In another sense, however, the attraction and fascination of these ancient civilizations of the New World are universal, and their study yields rewards for people of any background.

References

The following abbreviations are used in this section:

CIW   Carnegie Institution of Washington, Washington, D.C. Various publication series.

HMAI   *Handbook of Middle American Indians,* University of Texas Press, Austin.

INAH   Instituto Nacional de Antropologia e Historia de Mexico, Mexico City. Various publication series.

MARI   Middle American Research Institute, Tulane University, New Orleans. Various publications.

UCARF   *Contributions,* University of California Archaeological Research Facility, Berkeley.

Adams, R.E.W.
1991   *Prehistoric Mesoamerica.* Rev. ed. University of Oklahoma Press. Norman.

Adams, R.E.W., Hubert R. Robichaux, and Ruth Mathews
1997   Urban Centers, Construction Episodes, and Population Histories in the Three Rivers Region. *The Lowland Maya Regional Project Reports, No. 2.* The University of Texas at San Antonio.

Adams, R.E.W., and W. D. Smith
1977   Apocalyptic Visions: The Maya Collapse and Mediaeval Europe. *Archaeology* 30:292–301.

Aldred, Cyril
1965   *Egypt to the End of the Old Kingdom.* Thames and Hudson. London and New York.

Alva, Walter
1990   New Tomb of Royal Splendor. *National Geographic Magazine* 177(6):2–15.

Armillas, P.
1971   Gardens on Swamps. *Science* 174:653–661.

Aveni, A. F., E. E. Calnek, and H. Hartung
1988   Myth, Environment, and the Orientation of the Templo Mayor. *American Antiquity* 53:287–309.

Ball, J. W.
1985   Campeche, the Itza, and the Postclassic: A Study in Ethnohistorical Ar-
        chaeology. In J. A. Sabloff and E. W. Andrews V, eds., *Late Lowland
        Maya Civilization: Classic to Postclassic*, pp. 379–408. University of New
        Mexico Press. Albuquerque.

Bard, K. A.
1994   The Egyptian Predynastic: A Review of the Evidence. *Journal of Field
        Archaeology* 21(3):265–288.

Bauer, Brian
1991   Pacariqtambo and the Mythical Origins of the Inca. *Latin American An-
        tiquity* 2(1):7–26.

Beck, Coleen M.
1979   Ancient Roads on the North Coast of Peru. Ph.D. diss., University of
        California, Berkeley.

Benfer, R. A.
1990   The Preceramic Period Site of Paloma, Peru: Bioindications of Improv-
        ing Adaptation to Sedentism. *Latin American Antiquity* 1(4):284–318.

Blanton, R. E.
1978   *Monte Alban: Settlement Patterns at the Ancient Zapotec Capital.* Aca-
        demic Press. New York.
1983   Monte Alban in Period V. In Kent V. Flannery and Joyce Marcus, eds.,
        The Cloud People, pp. 281–282. Academic Press. New York.

Bricker, V.
1986   *A Grammar of Maya Hieroglyphs.* MARI Pub. 56.

Bruhns, Karen Olsen
1994   *Ancient South America.* Cambridge University Press. Cambridge.

Burger, R. L.
1992   *Chavin and the Origins of Andean Civilization.* Thames and Hudson.
        London and New York.

Campbell, L., and T. Kaufman
1993   A Decipherment of Epi-Olmec Hieroglyphic Writing. *Science*
        259:1703–1711.

Caso, A., and I. Bernal
1952   *Urnas de Oaxaca.* Memorias del Instituto de Antropologia e Historia de
        Mexico. Mexico City.

Chang, Kwang-chih
1977   *The Archaeology of Ancient China.* 3d ed. Yale University Press. New
        Haven.

1986   *The Archaeology of Ancient China.* 4th ed. Yale University Press. New Haven.

Childe, V. Gordon
1950   The Urban Revolution. *Town Planning Review* 21:3–17.

Coe, M. D.
1968   *America's First Civilization.* D. Van Nostrand. New York.

Coe, M. D., and R. A. Diehl
1980   *In the Land of the Olmec.* University of Texas Press. Austin.

Coggins, Clemency Chase
1979   A New Order and the Role of the Calendar: Some Characteristics of the Middle Classic Period at Tikal. In N. Hammond and G. R. Willey, eds., *Maya Archaeology and Ethnohistory*, pp. 38–50. University of Texas Press. Austin.
1992   *Artifacts from the Cenote of Sacrifice, Chichen Itza, Yucatan.* Memoir 10 (3), Peabody Museum of Archaeology and Ethnology. Harvard University. Cambridge.

Conklin, William J., and Michael E. Moseley
1988   The Patterns of Art and Power in the Early Intermediate Period. In Richard W. Keatinge, ed., *Peruvian Prehistory*, pp. 145–163. Cambridge University Press. Cambridge.

Conrad, Geoffrey W., and Arthur A. Demarest
1984   *Religion and Empire.* Cambridge University Press. Cambridge.

Cowgill, George
1988   Onward and Upward with Collapse. In Norman Yoffee and George Cowgill, eds., *The Collapse of Ancient States and Civilizations.* University of Arizona Press. Tucson.

Culbert, T. Patrick
1973   (ed.) *The Classic Maya Collapse.* University of New Mexico Press. Albuquerque.
1974   *The Lost Civilization: The Story of the Classic Maya.* Harper and Row. New York.

Culbert, T. P., L. J. Kosakowsky, R. E. Fry, and W. A. Haviland
1990   The Population of Tikal, Guatemala. In T. P. Culbert and D. S. Rice, eds., *Precolumbian Population History in the Maya Lowlands*, pp. 103–121. University of New Mexico Press. Albuquerque.

Dales, G. F.
1966   The Decline of the Harrapans. *Scientific American* 214(5):92–100.

Diaz del Castillo, Bernal
1956   *The Discovery and Conquest of Mexico.* Translated by A. P. Maudslay. Noonday Press. New York.

Diehl, R. A.
1983   *Tula, the Toltec Capital of Ancient Mexico.* Thames and Hudson. London.

Dillehay, Tom D.
1989   *Monte Verde: A Late Pleistocene Settlement in Chile.* Vol. 1. Smithsonian Institution Press. Washington, D.C.

Di Peso, Chas. C.
1974   *Casas Grandes.* 9 vols. Northland Press. Flagstaff, Arizona.

Donnan, Christopher B.
1964   An Early House from Chilca, Peru. *American Antiquity* 30:137–144.
1976   *Moche Art and Iconography.* UCLA Latin American Center Publication. Los Angeles.
1990   Masterworks of Art Reveal a Remarkable Pre-Inca World. *National Geographic Magazine* 177(6):16–33.

Drucker, Philip, Robert F. Heizer, and Robert J. Squier
1959   *Excavations at La Venta, Tabasco, 1955.* Bureau of American Ethnology Bulletin 170. Washington, D.C.

Duran, Diego
1964   *The Aztecs. The History of the Indies of New Spain.* Translated with notes by Doris Heyden and Fernando Horcasitas. Orion Press. New York.

Edey, Maitland A.
1975   *The Lost World of the Aegean.* Time-Life Books. New York.

Erickson, Clark L.
1993   The Social Organzation of Prehispanic Raised Field Agriculture in the Lake Titicaca Basin. In Vernon L. Scarborough and Barry L. Isaac, *Economic Aspects of Water Management in the Prehispanic New World*, pp. 369–426. Research in Economic Anthropology, Supplement No. 7. JAI Press. Greenwich, Connecticut, and London.

Fairservice, Walter
1971   *The Roots of Ancient India.* Macmillan. New York.
1991   G. L. Possehl's and M. H. Raval's *Harrapan Civilization and Rojdi.* Review article, *Journal of the American Oriental Society* 111(1):108–113.

Flannery, Kent V.
1983   The Legacy of the Early Urban Period. In Kent V. Flannery and Joyce Marcus, eds., *The Cloud People*, pp. 132–136. Academic Press. New York.

Flannery, Kent V., and Joyce Marcus
1983   (eds.) *The Cloud People.* Academic Press. New York.
1994   *Early Formative Pottery of the Valley of Oaxaca, Mexico.* Memoirs of the
        Museum of Anthropology, University of Michigan, No. 27. Ann Arbor.

Fung de Pineda, Rosa
1988   The Late Preceramic and Initial Period. In Richard W. Keatinge, ed.,
        Peruvian Prehistory, pp. 67–96. Cambridge University Press. Cam-
        bridge.

Garcia Cook, Angel
1981   The Historical Importance of Tlaxcala in the Cultural Development of
        the Central Highlands. In Victoria Bricker and Jeremy A. Sabloff, eds.,
        Supplement to the Handbook of Middle American Indians, Vol. 1, pp.
        244–276. University of Texas Press. Austin.

Garcilaso de la Vega
1966   *Royal Commentaries of the Incas and General History of Peru.* Translated
        by H. V. Livermore. University of Texas Press. Austin.

Gill, R. B.
1994   The Great Maya Droughts. Ph.D. diss., University of Texas, Austin.

Gorenstein, S. S., and H. P. Pollard
1983   *The Tarascan Civilization.* Vanderbilt University Publications in An-
        thropology. Nashville, Tennessee.

Graham, John A.
1978   *Abaj Takalik 1976: Exploratory Investigations. UCARF* Contributions
        No. 36.

Grove, David C.
1981   The Formative Period and the Evolution of Complex Culture. *HMAI,
        Supplement, Archaeology*, pp. 373–391.
1987   Chalcatzingo in a Broader Perspective. In D. C. Grove, ed., *Ancient
        Chalcatzingo.* University of Texas Press. Austin.
1992   The Olmec Legacy. *National Geographic Research and Exploration*
        8(2):148–165.

Haas, J., S. Pozorski, and T. Pozorski
1988   (eds.) *The Origins and Development of the Andean State.* Cambridge Uni-
        versity Press. Cambridge.

Hansen, R. D.
1991   The Road to Nakbe. *Natural History* (May): 8–14. The American Mu-
        seum of Natural History. New York.

Hassig, R.
1988   *Aztec Warfare; Imperial Expansion and Political Control.* University of Oklahoma Press. Norman.

Haury, E. W.
1937   A Pre-Spanish Rubber Ball from Arizona. *American Antiquity* 2:282–288.

Healan, D. M.
1974   Residential Architecture at Tula. In R. A. Diehl, ed., *Studies of Ancient Tollan*, pp. 16–24. Department of Anthropology, University of Missouri. Columbia.

Hirth, K.
1984   Xochicalco: Urban Growth and State Formation in Central Mexico. *Science* 225:579–586.
1995   Urbanism, Militarism, and Architectural Design. *Ancient Mesoamerica* 6(2):237–250.

Hoffecker, J. F., W. R. Powers, and T. Goebel
1993   The Colonization of Beringia and the Peopling of the New World. *Science* 259:46–53.

Hoffman, Michael A.
1979   *Egypt Before the Pharaohs.* Dorset. New York.

Hyslop, John
1984   *The Inka Road System.* Academic Press. New York.
1990   *Inka Settlement Planning.* University of Texas Press. Austin.

Isbell, William H.
1987   State Origins in the Ayacucho Valley, Central Highlands, Peru. In Jonathan Haas, Thomas Pozorski, and Shelia Pozorski, eds., *The Origins and Development of the Andean State*, pp. 83–90. Cambridge University Press. Cambridge.
1988   City and State in Middle Horizon Huari. In Richard W. Keatinge, ed., *Peruvian Prehistory*, pp. 164–189. Cambridge University Press. Cambridge.

Isbell, William H., and K. Schreiber
1978   Was Huari a State? *American Antiquity* 48(3):372–389.

Jimenez-Moreno, W.
1966   Los Imperios Prehispanicos de Mesoamerica. *Revista de la Sociedad Mexicana de Antropologia* 20:179–195.

Jones, C., and L. Satterthwaite Jr.
1982   *The Monuments and Inscriptions of Tikal: The Carved Monuments.* Tikal Report No. 33, Part A. The University Museum. Philadelphia.

Justeson, J. S., and T. Kaufman
1993   A Decipherment of Epi-Olmec Hieroglyphic Writing. *Science* 259: 1703–1711.

Kenyon, Kathleen
1957   *Digging Up Jericho*. Benn. London.

Keys, David
1994   How Earth and Jupiter Are Alike. *Toronto Globe and Mail* (21 July 1994).

Kolata, Alan L.
1983   The South Andes. In J. D. Jennings, ed., *Ancient South Americans*, pp. 240–285. Freeman. New York.
1986   The Agricultural Foundations of the Tiwanaku State: A View from the Heartland. *American Antiquity* 51(4):748–762.
1991   The Technology and Organization of Agricultural Production in the Tiwanaku State. *Latin American Antiquity* 2(2):99–125.

Kramer, S. N.
1963   *The Sumerians*. University of Chicago Press. Chicago.

Kroeber, A. L.
1963   *Configurations of Culture Growth*. University of California Press. Berkeley.

Krotser, P., and G. R. Krotser
1973   The Life Style of El Tajín. *American Antiquity* 38:199–205.

Lloyd, Seton
1978   *The Archaeology of Mesopotamia*. Thames and Hudson. London.

Lowe, J.W.G.
1985   *The Dynamics of Apocalypse: A Systems Simulation of the Classic Maya Collapse*. University of New Mexico Press. Albuquerque.

Lynch, Thomas
1983   The Paleo-Indians. In Jesse D. Jennings, ed., *Ancient South Americans*, pp. 87–137. Freeman. New York.

MacLeod, M. J.
1973   *Spanish Central America*. University of California Press. Berkeley.

MacNeish, Richard S.
1992   *The Origins of Agriculture and Settled Life*. University of Oklahoma Press. Norman.

Marcus, Joyce
1980   Zapotec Writing. *Scientific American* (February), pp. 50–64.

1983a Stone Monuments and Tomb Murals of Monte Alban IIIa. In Kent V. Flannery and Joyce Marcus, eds., *The Cloud People*, pp. 137–143. Academic Press. New York.

1983b Teotihuacan Visitors on Monte Alban Monuments and Murals. In Kent V. Flannery and Joyce Marcus, eds., *The Cloud People*, pp. 175–181. Academic Press. New York.

1983c Aztec Military Campaigns Against the Zapotecs: The Documentary Evidence. In Kent V. Flannery and Joyce Marcus, eds., *The Cloud People*, pp. 314–318. Academic Press. New York.

1992 *Mesoamerican Writing Systems.* Princeton University Press. Princeton.

Marcus, J., and Wm. J. Folan
1994 Una estela más del siglo V y nueva informacion sobre Pata de Jaguar, gobernante de Calakmul, Campeche, en el siglo VII. *Gaceta Universitaria* 4(15–16):21–26. Campeche, Mexico.

Mason, J. Alden
1968 *The Ancient Civilizations of Peru.* Penguin Books. London.

Matos Moctezuma, Eduardo
1988 *The Great Temple of the Aztecs.* Thames and Hudson. New York.

Meadows, D. H., D. L. Meadows, J. Randers, and W. W. Behrens III
1972 *Limits to Growth.* Universe Books. New York.

Mellart, James
1967 *Çatal Hüyük, a Neolithic Town in Anatolia.* Thames and Hudson. London.
1975 *The Neolithic of the Near East.* Charles Scribner's Sons. New York.

Millon, Clara
1973 Painting, Writing, and Polity at Teotihuacan, Mexico. *American Antiquity* 38:294–314.

Millon, Rene
1981 Teotihuacan. In *HMAI*, Supplement, Archaeology, pp. 198–243.
1988 The Last Years of Teotihuacan Dominance. In N. Yoffee and G. L. Cowgill, eds., *The Collapse of Ancient States and Civilizations.* University of Arizona Press. Tucson.

Morley, S. G., G. W. Brainerd, and R. J. Sharer
1983 *The Ancient Maya.* 4th ed. Stanford University Press. Stanford.

Morris, Craig, and Donald E. Thompson
1985 *Huanuco Pampa: An Inca City and Its Hinterland.* Thames and Hudson. London.

Moseley, M. E.
1975   *The Maritime Foundations of Andean Civilization.* Cummings. Menlo Park, California.

1992   *The Incas and Their Ancestors.* Thames and Hudson. New York and London.

Murra, John V.
1962   Cloth and Its Functions in the Inca State. *American Anthropologist* 64(4):710–728.

Nials, F. L., E. E. Deeds, M. E. Moseley, S. G. Pozorski, T. G. Pozorski, and R. A. Feldman
1979   El Niño: The Catastrophic Flooding of Coastal Peru. *Field Museum of Natural History Bulletin* 50(7):4–14 (Part I); and 50(8):4–10 (Part II).

Ortloff, C. R., M. E. Moseley, and R. A. Feldman
1982   Hydraulic Engineering Aspects of the Chimu Chicama-Moche Inter-valley Canal. *American Antiquity* 47(3):572–595.

Paddock, J.
1966   *Ancient Oaxaca.* Stanford University Press. Stanford.

Paul, Anne
1990   *Paracas Ritual Attire.* University of Oklahoma Press. Norman.
1991   (ed.) *Paracas Art and Architecture.* University of Iowa Press. Iowa City.

Platt, Colin
1979   *The English Medieval Town.* McKay. New York.

Pozorski, Shelia
1982   Subsistence Systems in the Chimu State. In Michael E. Moseley and Kent C. Day, eds. *Chan Chan: Andean Desert City,* pp. 177–196. University of New Mexico Press. Albuquerque.
1988   Theocracy vs. Militarism: The Significance of the Casma Valley in Understanding Early State Formation. In J. Haas, S. Pozorski, and T. Pozorski, eds., *The Origins and Development of the Andean State,* pp. 15–30. Cambridge University Press. Cambridge.

Pozorski, Shelia, and Thomas Pozorski
1987   *Early Settlement and Subsistence in the Casma Valley.* University of Iowa Press. Iowa City.

Proskouriakoff, T.
1960   Historical Implications of a Pattern of Dates at Piedras Negras, Guatemala. *American Antiquity* 25:454–475.

Raikes, R. L.
1964   The End of the Ancient Cities of the Indus. *American Anthropologist*
        66:284–299.

Rattray, Evelyn C.
1987   The Merchants Barrio, Teotihuacan. Preliminary Report submitted to
        INAH and Instituto de Investigaciones Antropologicas, Universidad
        Autonoma de Mexico. Mexico.

Robichaux, Hubert R.
1990   The Hieroglyphic Texts of Rio Azul, Guatemala. M.A. thesis, Univer-
        sity of Texas at San Antonio. San Antonio.

Rowe, John H.
1946   Inca Culture at the Time of the Spanish Conquest. In Julian Steward,
        ed., *The Handbook of South American Indians*. Vol. 5, *The Andean Civi-
        lizations*, pp. 183–330. Bulletin of the Bureau of American Ethnology,
        No. 146. Washington, D.C.

Roys, Ralph L.
1957   *The Political Geography of the Yucatan Maya*. Carnegie Institution of
        Washington, Pub. 613. Washington, D.C.
1962   Literary Sources for the History of Mayapan. In H.E.D. Pollock et al.,
        eds., *Mayapan, Yucatan, Mexico*. Carnegie Institution of Washington,
        Pub. 619. Washington, D.C.

Rust, W. F., and R. J. Sharer
1988   Olmec Settlement Data from La Venta, Tabasco. *Science* 242:102–104.

Sahagun, Bernadino de
1950–   *The Florentine Codex: General History of the Things of New Spain*. 12 vols.
1970   Translated by C. E. Dibble and A.J.O. Anderson. School of American
        Research and University of Utah Press. Provo.

Sanders, W. T.
1970   The Population of the Teotihuacan Valley, the Basin of Mexico, and the
        Central Mexican Symbiotic Region in the Sixteenth Century. In W. T.
        Sanders, A. Kovar, T. Charlton, and R. A. Diehl, eds., *The Teotihuacan
        Valley Project, Final Report*, vol. 1, pp. 385–457. Occcasional Papers in
        Anthropology, No. 3. Department of Anthropology, Pennsylvania State
        University. University Park.

Sanders, W. T., J. R. Parsons, and R. S. Santley
1979   *The Basin of Mexico: Ecological Processes in the Evolution of a Civilization*.
        Academic Press. New York.

Sanders, W. T., and Barbara J. Price
1968   *Mesoamerica: The Evolution of a Civilization.* Random House. New York.

Saul, F. P.
1973   *Disease in the Maya Area: The Pre-Columbian Evidence.* In T. Patrick Culbert, ed., *The Classic Maya Collapse,* pp. 301–324. University of New Mexico Press. Albuquerque.

Sawyer, Alan R.
1961   Paracas and Nazca Iconography. In S. K. Lothrop, ed. *Essays in Pre-Columbian Art and Archaeology,* pp. 269–298. Harvard University Press. Cambridge.

Scarborough, V. L.
1994   Maya Water Management. *National Geographic Research and Exploration* 10(2):184–199.

Schreiber, Katherine J.
1988   From State to Empire: The Expansion of Wari Outside the Ayacucho Basin. In J. Haas, S. Pozorski, and T. Pozorski, eds., *The Origins and Development of the Andean State,* pp. 83–96. Cambridge University Press. Cambridge.

Silverman, Helaine
1988   Cahuachi: Non-Urban Cultural Complexity on the South Coast of Peru. *Journal of Field Archaeology* 15(4):403–430.

Simmel, Georg
1950   *The Sociology of Georg Simmel.* Translated, edited, and with introduction by Kurt H. Wolff. Free Press. New York.

Stein, G., and M. S. Rothman
1994   (eds.) *Chiefdoms and Early States in the Near East.* Prehistory Press. Madison, Wisconsin.

Stuart, G. E.
1993   The Carved Stela from La Mojarra, Veracruz, Mexico. *Science* 259:1700–1701.

Topic, Theresa L.
1982   The Early Intermediate Period and Its Legacy. In Michael E. Moseley and Kent C. Day, eds., *Chan Chan: Andean Desert City,* pp. 255–284. University of New Mexico Press. Albuquerque.

Topic, John, and Theresa Topic
1987   The Archaeological Investigation of Andean Militarism: Some Cautionary Observations. In Jonathan Haas, Shelia Pozorski, and Thomas

Pozorski, eds., *The Origins and Development of the Andean State.* Cambridge University Press. Cambridge.

Wheeler, Mortimer
1966   *Civilizations of the Indus Valley and Beyond.* McGraw-Hill. New York.

Wilkerson, S.J.K.
1987   *El Tajín: A Guide for Visitors.* The Museum of Xalapa. Veracruz, Mexico.

Wooley, C. L.
1954   *Excavations at Ur.* Benn. London.

Wright, H. T.
1994   Prestate Political Formations. In G. Stein and M. S. Rothman, eds., *Chiefdoms and Early States in the Near East,* pp. 67–84. Preshistory Press. Madison, Wisconsin.

Wright, H. T., and G. A. Johnson
1975   Population, Exchange and Early State Formation in Southwestern Iran. *American Anthropologist* 77:267–289.

About the Book and Author

In this concise, yet sweeping look at the origins and development of ancient New World civilizations, Richard Adams provides a superb introductory overview of these unique and fascinating cultures. Incorporating the latest breakthroughs in the study of the cultures of Mesoamerica and the Andes, Adams examines the development of the Olmec, Maya, Aztec, and Inca peoples, among others, from simple agricultural societies to urban civilizations with complex transportation networks, distinct social hierarchies, rich artistic and religious traditions, and writing systems that have defied anthropological investigation until recently.

The question of why these thriving cultures collapsed so suddenly when faced with the European conquest is explored, as are comparisons with ancient Old World civilizations of the Middle East and Asia.

Richard E.W. Adams is professor of anthropology at the University of Texas. His many scholarly publications include *Prehistoric Mesoamerica.*

Index